BULTMANN
and
CHRISTIAN FAITH

BULTMANN
and
CHRISTIAN FAITH

by
RENÉ MARLÉ, S.J.

Translated by
THEODORE DUBOIS

NEWMAN PRESS

Westminster, Md.　　　New York, N.Y.　　　Glen Rock, N.J.

Amsterdam　　　Toronto

A Newman Press edition, originally published under the title *Bultmann et la foi Chrétienne,* © Editions Auber-Montaigne 1966, Paris, France.

NIHIL OBSTAT:
Robert E. Hunt, S.T.D.
Censor Librorum

IMPRIMATUR:
✠ Thomas A. Boland, S.T.D.
Archbishop of Newark

October 24, 1967

The Nihil Obstat and Imprimatur are official declarations that a book or pamphlet is free of doctrinal or moral error. No implication is contained therein that those who have granted the Nihil Obstat and Imprimatur agree with the contents, opinions or statements expressed.

Library of Congress
Catalog Card Number: 68-16663

Published by Newman Press
Editorial Office: 304 W. 58th St., N.Y., N.Y. 10019
Business Office: Westminster, Maryland 21157

Printed and bound in the
United States of America

Contents

Foreword

Rudolf Bultmann is the focal point of most of the theological research and controversy of our times. He has posed unavoidable problems and has proposed solutions that have captivated some thinkers and raised the indignation of others. Anyone who feels the need of re-thinking his faith in contemporary terms, must situate himself in relation to Bultmann.

Since 1956, Father Marlé has devoted himself to the fundamental study of Bultmann's interpretation of the New Testament. The recent publication of an updated and augmented edition of his work furnishes the basis for this present volume. He has deliberately omitted the technical apparatus and some developments of interest to specialists which exceded the purpose of this present work.

This book furnishes an excellent introduction to the thought of the great German theologian, and, at the same time, it indicates his limits and his serious ambiguities.

Abbreviations

Ev. Joh.   = *Das Evangelium des Johannes.*
G.V.   = *Glauben und Verstehen.*
K.M.   = *Kerygma und Mythos.*
                (Eng. tr.: *Kerygma and Myth,* ed. H. W. Bartsch.
                Harper Torchbooks, 1961.)
R.B.   = *Revue biblique.*
R.G.G.   = *Die Religion in Geschichte und Gegenwart.*
R.H.P.R. = *Revue d'histoire et de philosophie religieuse.*
R.S.R.   = *Recherches de science religieuse.*
Th.L.   = *Theologische Literaturzeitung.*
Th.N.T.   = *Theologie des Neuen Testaments.*
                (Eng. tr.: *Theology of the New Testament,* 2 vols.
                Scribner.)
Z.N.T.W. = *Zeitschrift für die neutestamentliche Wissenschaft.*
Z.Th.K.   = *Zeitschrift für Theologie und Kirche.*
Zw.Z.   = *Zwischen den Zeiten.*

Our references to:
         R. Bultmann, *Geschichte der synoptischen Tradition,*
         (Eng. tr.: *History of the Synoptic Tradition.* Harper,
         1963.)
         R. Bultmann, *Theologie des Neuen Testaments,*
         F. Gogarten, *Entmythologisierung und Kirche,*
are taken from the first edition of these works. Those from:
         Kerygma und Mythos I,
         Die Religion in Geschichte und Gegenwart,
are from the second edition. Those from:
         Das Evangelium des Johannes,
are from the 1952 edition, which is numbered 12th in the
Commentary.

Introduction

Rudolf Bultmann has long been known for his critical labors on the New Testament and especially for his important contribution to the elaboration of the method known as *Formgeschichte*.[1] Since World War II, he has attained major prominence not only in exegesis, his field of specialization, but also in theology in general. Today, and rightfully so, he is attracting the attention of everyone interested in the movement of modern ideas.

Bultmann was born in 1884; he produced his major works between 1920 and 1960. Today he is a classic in theology. His thought can no longer be ignored, and it has retained all of its actuality. He remains the major reference in numerous debates. He asked the questions, and we must proceed through his work in order to understand the research and discussions that are presently being carried on.

Nevertheless, we still find that his work is generally known only in a fragmentary way. This book intends to introduce and situate his work and, at the same time, to offer a critical reaction to its limits and more fundamental insufficiencies.

Chapter I localizes Bultmann in the perspective of contemporary Protestant theology.

Chapter II's study of the problem of demythologizing, and of Bultmann's project of existentialist interpretation, should enable the reader to grasp the preoccupation of this exegesis which has more than once appeared scandalous, but which nonetheless corresponds to a constructive outline.

[1] Cf. *infra*, pp. 10ff.

Bultmann's program of demythologizing and existentialist interpretation occurs within a theology of the Word of God that must be studied in itself. If the liberal theologians of the nineteenth and the beginning of the twentieth centuries can be considered, above all, as theologians of the religious experience, Bultmann deliberately lists himself among the theologians of the Word. The important renewal in Protestantism that occurred right after World War II is due to these latter theologians.

Chapter III brings into relief the broad lines of Bultmann's theology of the Word of God.

Chapter IV traces the significance and meaning of the Old Testament in Bultmann's interpretation of Christian faith. Nor can this be a minor question, if it is true that the interpretation of Scripture—which is the object of all of Bultmann's work—always looks back to a certain understanding of the relation between the two Testaments.

Finally, Chapter V describes the distinctive traits of Bultmann's ecclesiology. It is not necessary to underline the importance of this question today. Our examination of it concludes a work that does not pretend to furnish a complete statement of Bultmann's thought; but we hope that by following certain major axes, we have gone right to its center.

We might say that we have entered the realm of fundamental options when we sketched our reflective criticisms at the end of each chapter (except for the first which is only an historical introduction). These proceed from the conviction that Bultmann is not simply a scandalous author who is to be rejected, nor the absolute master who has found the only possible solution to problems posed today. He is, rather, a demanding mind who incites us to continue our reflection and research.

CHAPTER ONE

Bultmann In Perspective

Liberal Theology and Dialectical Theology

Rudolf Bultmann is a sensitive point in contemporary Protestant theology and a scandal to some people. A prophetic breath seems to have aroused, if not all of evangelical theology, at least an important part of its most influential and most eminent representatives. We might have hoped that the harmful work of liberal criticism had come to an end, though not by a panic-stricken and fragile recourse to congealed orthodoxy or by an unthinking pietism, but rather by the rediscovery of the stupendous actuality of the Word of God and of the echo it found in the spirit of the Reformers. Karl Barth stands in first rank among the witnesses and the workers of this renaissance. Bultmann, however, has brought everything into question again. He believes that the problems posed by liberal theology have never really been resolved, although the questions involved were very serious ones. If we ignore them any longer, it will be impossible for the intellectuals of our age, whose exigencies were formulated by nineteenth-century criticism, to accept the New Testament message. It may be true that in meticulously applying the principles of modern scientific criticism to the New Testament, nineteenth-century theology did not manage to save the New Testament message from this criticism's dissolving work. But it is equally incorrect to think that these intellectuals will be satisfied for very long by a "non-critical" return to the scriptural texts; nor can such a procedure consider itself more faithful to the scriptural texts themselves. Isn't it our primary obligation, he asks, to faithfully investigate, with every means at our disposal, what Scripture properly signifies?

Undoubtedly, the confusion would have not been so great if this importunate call had come from one of the voices who never knew or wanted to recognize all that was valuable and great in the theological renewal that followed World War I. Yet Bultmann, as we know, was not only sympathetic to this renewal, but in the beginning actively collaborated with it. He is often cited with K. Barth, E. Thurneysen, F. Gogarten, and others, as one of the founders and most remarkable representatives of the group identified with "dialectical theology." He has never thought it necessary to correct or retract the positions he defended alongside of his old-time friends.

It is significant that from 1924 on, at the same time as he was heralding the new theological movement, he continued to respect all of liberal theology's undeniable discoveries.[1] He declared that it particularly had formed theologians to criticism, "in other words to liberty and to truth." "We, the heirs of liberal theology," he explained, "could never have become or remained theologians if we had not encountered the seriousness of radical veracity in liberal theology; we feel that the work of orthodox academic thelogy is an exercise in compromise in which we would only have been interiorly broken." He has never wanted to detract anything from the remarkable contribution of this historico-critical theology, or to deny anything of the spirit that gave it life.

His only reproach to liberal theology was that it had understood poorly the very meaning of the critical work to which it gave itself with such ability and conscientiousness, insofar as it thought that it could directly attain the proper object of faith. It forgot that God's revelation cannot be a mere historical element, no more than can a phenomenon of nature, that God is not a "datum," that his

[1] Cf. "Die liberale Theologie und die jüngste theologische Bewegung" in *G.V.* I, pp. 1ff.

Word always presents itself to us as a "scandal," that, far from coming at any time within the grasp of man, it always represents instead "the total suppression (*Aufhebung*) of man, his negation, his being put in question, the judgment made in his regard." It is easy to recognize in these statements some of the themes of Karl Barth's *Römerbrief* and other earlier articles, texts that Bultmann has each time made his own. And it is important to notice Bultmann's preoccupation from this time on: that, along with the profound religious intuitions that engendered dialectical theology, it is also necessary to accept, with as much respect, the considerable amount that is valuable in the heritage which liberal theology left us. To do this, one need only be sufficiently conscious of the meaning proper to each of these theological endeavors and of their mutual complementarity.

Moreover, at the same time as he was criticizing liberal theology according to the principles of dialectical theology, or rather as he was denouncing the theologically erroneous meaning that liberal theology had given to its work, Bultmann was careful to emphasize that his criticism pertained only to the orientation of this theology as a whole. "Several theologians," he indicated, "worked on themes that were to bring them to surpass themselves"; and he mentions above all the name of his teacher, W. Herrmann, as well as "the great aporetician of liberal theology, E. Troeltsch." Finally, he points out that theologians belonging to the circle of dialectical theology have themselves come from liberalism, and that this was not a matter of chance.

On the other hand, from 1922 on, praise was not the only thing he addressed to Karl Barth regarding the second edition of the *Römerbrief* in the review *Christliche Welt*. He declared that he did not at all agree with the conception of faith that Barth developed, whereby Pauline faith—true Christian faith—has no relation whatsoever with consciousness. Doesn't Barth, he asks, too hastily compare consciousness and the process of interiorization proper to it with the clear and distinct ideas in which it can be projected? Certainly, in this simple recension, Bultmann was not trying to judge all the principles of Barthian thelogy. But when he tells us that he does not feel comfortable "in the consequences of Barth's ideas on the meaning of faith and revelation," aren't we correct to underline the fundamental character of the divergencies between these two theologians as early as this time? And when Bultmann basically denounces in Barth an exaggerated supernaturalism, exegetically unjustified and actually proceeding from a false idea of transcendence and of the supernatural, can't we recognize already the most important questions concerning which these two dialectical theologians will not cease opposing each other?

During this same period, Bultmann opposed Barth not only in these fundamental ideas of theology but also in questions of method. He accused him of having "done violence" to the Epistle to the Romans and to Paul. And by this, Bultmann doesn't mean to criticize merely certain particulars of Barth's treatment, but to set himself against a method that compromises "clear understanding of the reality which is really signified." Barth, according to Bultmann, does not respect historical and philological criticism sufficiently. It is not that he fails to use it, but that it should be used primarily. It prevents us from imagining that Paul's thought is expressed in exactly the same way on every page that he wrote, and it also prevents us from using certain formulas merely as a springboard for stating our own ideas.

Bultmann feels that if we want to be faithful to the thought of an author, it is absolutely necessary to be attentive to the things that influenced him, to the "contradictions" or "tensions" that are internal to his work. This includes summits of thought, but also weaknesses, "high points" and "low points." A truly penetrating criticism should show "where and how the thing that is really signified is formulated," and should extract the real thought of the author from the more or less successful expressions that translate it. In fact, criticism "can never be too radical," but it will enable us to throw into relief the transcendence of that to which the written word is witnessing, with regard to the document itself and with regard to its author.

Analogous remarks, but more precise ones, accompany Bultmann's review in 1926 of Karl Barth's short work, *Die Auferstehung der Toten*,[2] a commentary on the First Epistle to the Corinthians centering on Chapter 15. To furnish a valuable commentary for this text as for any other, Bultmann believes that criticism

[2] Reprinted in *G.V.* I, pp. 38ff.

should not be used only sporadically and only when it seems impossible to take the text as it is. Rather, it should never be abandoned and should comprehend the whole document, so that behind the multiplicity of formulas it can consider the weaknesses as well as the successful turns of phrase and thus discover the very intention of the author. An author cannot but express himself in the thought patterns of the world to which he belongs. And since it is not simply a matter of opposing statements attributed solely to the author with others attributed solely to the ideas of the times, there can be no valuable exegesis that does not rest primarily on a continual criticism. Bultmann considers Barth's thought to be unfaithful to the text on which it comments, but he also thinks that Barth's elaboration on a conceptual plane is insufficient to express satisfactorily those things he did glimpse correctly.

It is unnecessary for us to pursue in any further detail the objections which Bultmann makes to Barth and the positions that will bring these two theologians to follow ever more divergent paths; nor is it necessary for us to make an inventory of the themes of liberal theology that Bultmann has rehabilitated in his work, nor to list the problems he seeks to solve in its wake. The problem of demythologizing, which will comprise part of our study, furnishes an adequate example of the fidelity he has always manifested for the preoccupations of liberal theology.

We need not be overly surprised by the great divergencies among the early adherents to dialectical theology. This theology never intended to define itself as a closed doctrine with well-established theses. Barth himself declared that the dialectical theologians in no way pretended to be advancing a new theology to replace existing theologies, but intended merely to furnish them with a marginal gloss. During a theological conference held at Eisenach in 1927, when he spoke on the question of "The Meaning of 'Dialectical Theology' for New Testament Science," [3] Bultmann stated at the beginning of his discourse that the term "dialectical theology" does not designate a system with a set of dogmatic propositions on which, according to circumstances, New Testament science should depend; it is not even a method of research

---

[3] "Die Bedeutung der 'dialektischen Theologie' für die neutestamentliche Wissenschaft" reprinted in *G.V.* I, pp. 114ff.

which would, for example, be substituted for the historical method; rather, it signifies merely a certain way of thinking and of speaking, a certain way of being, of understanding oneself and of conducting oneself in face of reality. "The big word 'dialectical theology' signifies, in short, considering the historicity of human being."

According to Bultmann's thought, it is proper to dialectical theology to refer all our ideas and all our investigations of sources and documents to this "historicity" which constitutes us, and where all our activities, as well as all our encounters and all our discoveries, find their meaning. Far from governing a system, it implies always asking questions about everything that science can discover or that speculation can develop. What it defines is the attitude of the exegete who is confronted again and again to let himself be judged by the living Word. But although it may furnish a new motive for research and may give to New Testament science (as indeed to science in general) its final meaning, it can in no way be substituted for historical and critical research which should be developed without hindrance and without limitation on its own ground and with its own methods.

These last reflections show us that Bultmann obtains an original place in the movement referred to as dialectical theology, not only by his research in a particular area, but equally by the very precise meaning he gives to this movement. In defining all dialectical theology primarily as "considering the historicity of human being," he announces the direction in which he himself will develop his own theology with an ever more advanced technical perfection and, in particular, the elements which he will borrow from the existential philosophies, especially that of Heidegger.

The History of Literary Forms (Form-Criticism)

While Bultmann was stressing the importance of problems raised by liberal criticism, he did not mention the transformation he himself would accomplish. His reflections on the fundamental principles of dialectical theology indicated above merely show the direction that all his future work will follow. His first important work was a *History of the Synoptic Tradition;* [4] it appeared in 1921, one year before the second edition of Karl Barth's *Römerbrief.* This publication placed Bultmann among the founders of the *Formgeschichtliche Schule* (the Form-Criticism School) which studied the history of literary forms. With this precise orientation in his research, he joins the advocates of dialectical theology. It defines the manner in which he will surpass liberal criticism, while remaining faithful to all its demands. And it will remain the project of his entire work.

The fact that several exegetes produced a new method for research in the New Testament texts was due not to any desire to cause a revolution, but rather to their desire to answer problems that had remained unresolved up to that time. That several authors, without working together, should produce a new exegetical method step-by-step in works that appeared simultaneously and should in this way form a new "school," clearly indicates that whatever their respective originality they were answering problems raised by the situation in which science found itself at the time.

The works of Holtzmann and Weizsäcker dominate modern "independent" criticism of the Synoptic gospels. They got rid of Tübingen's fragile constructions and of Strauss' mythical theory, and they gave Mark's gospel priority over those of Matthew and Luke. Weizsäcker showed that besides the common source of gospel narrations which we find in Mark, we must admit that the Synoptic authors also used a second source, one composed of discourses, which appears with individual differences in Matthew and Luke. This, of course, is the "Double-Source Theory" which still today is considered by many to be the basis of studies into the Synoptic problem.[5] At least, it is considered as such by the founders of the Form-Criticism School.

[4] *Geschichte der synoptischen Tradition* (Göttingen, 1921).

[5] Cf. P. Benoit, "Réflexions sur la 'formgeschichtliche Methode'" (1946), in *Exégèse et théologie* I, (Paris, 1961), pp. 25-61. J. Weiss goes so far as to say that Mark's priority has been scientifically demonstrated (cf. L. Perriraz, *Histoire de la Théologie protestante aux XVIII° et XIX° siècles* II, [Neuchâtel, 1951], p. 130). Today, however, not all scholars agree with this opinion.

At the beginning of his *History of the Synoptic Tradition,* Bultmann introduces his purpose by citing Holtzmann and recalling the contribution which criticism made when it discovered that Mark's gospel is anterior to those of Matthew and Luke. But, at the same time, he shows how it is possible to draw unwarranted conclusions from this solid result. Basing themselves on the second gospel, some interpreters had considered themselves justified in using this primitive document as a setting for a history of the life of Jesus. It is an illusion that was quickly denounced, and Bultmann considers Wrede's work, *The Messianic Secret,* important because it definitively closes off this false track. Wrede maintains that the gospel of Mark doesn't give us a history of Jesus' life, but rather that its construction is based on theological reflection, and that this theological reflection was furnished by the faith of the Christian community in whose midst Mark wrote his gospel.

According to Wrede, the agony at Gethsemani, the flight of the disciples and certain other aspects would be incomprehensible if Jesus had revealed himself as the Messiah, if he had foretold his sufferings, if he had planned to die when he went to Jerusalem. His death confused and troubled all his disciples. It was only by means of their paschal faith that they began to proclaim him as Messiah. And in order to explain a messianic life which had not appeared to be messianic, they had to take recourse in the thesis of a progressive manifestation—veiled and mysterious, confided in secret—that he really was Messiah. In other words, according to Wrede, apologetic and kerygmatic needs brought the community to reinterpret the entire life of Jesus with an intention entirely contrary to that of collecting different episodes that would truly preserve his historical life. This, at least, could be the only way that Mark's gospel could be understood.

Bultmann remarks that although it is true that Wrede anticipates some of the essential intuitions of the Form-Criticism School, his importance consists especially in that he blocks off the direction in which New Testament studies were heading, and his work could not help but cause new questions to rise immediately. Taking into account the new fact that Mark's gospel had a prehistory, the purpose of these questions was to know more precisely just what documents could enable us to know this prehistory and how these documents, in turn, should be listed and evaluated.

J. Weiss, basing himself on Papias, thought that he had found in Mark a record of Peter's remembrances. But this attempt turned out to be much too simplistic, so criticism turned instead to pure literary analysis. In the same way as the Graf-Welhausen School had done for the Old Testament, scholars cut the New Testament texts into an infinity of pieces to identify the innumerable sources. The names of Wendling, Spitta, Zahn, and others, belong to these works whose results certainly were not proportionate to the sum of effort expended.

Scholars came to realize that other means besides the purely literary comparison and classification of texts were possible. At the beginning of the nineteenth century, the first critical studies on the Gospel (Herder, Krummacher, Gieseler and even Schleiermacher) had called attention to the oral phase which preceded the written Gospel texts. In other words, the Gospel should be considered as the witness of a living tradition rather than as a document given immediately in its definitive form. But, because they did not have a solid literary criticism on which to base themselves, this intuition could not be transformed into a serious study of tradition considered in its light. More recently, a study much as A. Jülicher's on *The Parables of Jesus* (1889) had tried to extract what tradition had added to the original words of Jesus in order to illustrate them or to render them more comprehensible. But Jülicher's work regarded a very particular field, and his criticism was limited in its very principle by his idea that the point of departure of every parable was really an historical saying of Jesus.

Wellhausen's studies on the Synoptics and especially the ideas that he formulated in his *Introduction to the First Three Gospels* (1905) were, even according to Bultmann, much more important for the evolution of research. Not only did Wellhausen extend to Matthew and to Luke (and therefore to the Q-source) Wrede's principles regarding the influence of the early Christian community's theology on its presentation of the historical "given," but he also showed more clearly how the work of redaction had affected pieces that originally were isolated and belonged to different layers of the tradition. Therefore, it became more important to determine the age of these individual layers than to determine the age of the documents in which they were contained.

Two factors whose origins are closely related helped to orient research in this direction. These are the perspectives opened by the history of religions and by H. Gunkel's work on the Old Testament. The history of comparative religions attracted attention to the number of dynamic factors that could have intervened in the life of the community and, therefore, in the development of tradition. This is the way that W. Bousset, in his renowned *Kyrios Christos* (1913), shed light on the capital influence that the cult addressed to the Kyrios on primitive tradition. In the same work he asked, without however developing his idea any farther, that "an entirely new method" be undertaken "which would, above all, consider style, and which would be directed to research into the laws of oral tradition." However, the scholars of the Comparative-Religions School occupied themselves primarily with comparing the form and content of the New Testament with that of analogous documents furnished by the surrounding world. The Christian tradition, seen in itself, with its formation and development, was not the direct object of their research.

While the history of comparative religions opened perspectives rich with promise on Christian origins, H. Gunkel's work on *Genesis* (1901) outlined quite a new exegetical and historical method which was soon widely acclaimed. In his famous commentary, Gunkel gave the oral tradition an important place. According to him, it consisted of isolated elements which tended to form themselves in cycles. He insisted, above all, that it is necessary to determine the place and the meaning of the documents in the life of the people, the *Sitz im Leben*. And it is these ideas which, transposed to the New Testament, were to regulate the work of the Form-Criticism School.[6]

---

[6] Bultmann wrote in his introduction to the *History of the Synoptic Tradition* that we must apply to the various gospel pericopes "the consideration relative to the history-of-forms which has been attempted in other fields" (p. 2). He is alluding not only to Gunkel, but also to analogous studies in profane literature (Norden, Wendland, for example, whom he cites on p. 4). We may also consult, on this same subject, P. Benoit, *"Réflexions sur la 'formgeschichtliche Methode',"* loc. cit., p. 485.

Indeed, if we had to define in a few words what is most characteristic of this new school whose representatives are far from holding identical positions and whose unfortunate name is quite untranslatable, we would say that it is the desire to establish, on the basis of a critical analysis of the different elements which constitute the New Testament writings, the history of the tradition which is fixed in them and which alone enables us to interpret them correctly. K. L. Schmidt writes that "research into the oral tradition whose content is fixed in the gospels in a literary way is the fundamental point of view which commands this historical study of forms." [7] Bultmann tells us that "this distinction between tradition and redaction is essential, as it is brought out in K. L. Schmidt's book, *Der Rahmen der Geschichte Jesu* (1919); it is a fundamental and decisive criticism of the previous opinion which, though ingeniously expressed by Spitta, had ended in definitive failure."

In the same year as K. L. Schmidt published his book, M. Dibelius wrote his short work, *Formgeschichte des Evangeliums;* he set forth precisely what he considered to be the new method's principles, and he began to apply them to the different elements of the Gospel tradition. Dibelius proposed, first of all, to separate the "pericopes," those elements in our gospels which originally were isolated. These pericopes, in turn, belong to determined literary groups (or "forms") whose origin and development must be studied. To accomplish this, Dibelius proceeded deductively, using the "offices," the functions and needs of the community, as a point of departure, and ending with the literary forms which should answer them. By his study, he hoped to obtain a solution regarding the principle, rather than detailed treatment, of the gospels' entire content.

When Bultmann published his *History of the Synoptic Tradition* two years later (1921), he declared that he was following in the furrow plowed by K. L. Schmidt and M. Dibelius. But he is more ambitious than they, because he intends to accomplish an exhaustive analysis of all the Gospel pericopes. Above all, he is not content to merely set forth working principles, as Dibelius had

---

[7] "Formgeschichte," in *R.G.G.* II, col. 638.

done, by studying, for their own sake, the major forms in which the Gospel tradition was transmitted and fixed; rather, he seeks to establish the history of each pericope and, from there, to discover the laws governing the dynamic movement of tradition. While Dibelius' method is mostly deductive, or "constructive," Bultmann's is rather "analytic" and inductive. And we can note that if Bultmann uses analysis to determine the pericopes' *Sitz im Leben,* "the place where they appear and are treated in the community," then the "form" of these pericopes is understood to the degree that they are correctly situated. He further states that if, in his work, the analysis of each individual pericope precedes the view of the whole for each of the major literary groups he studies, it is only in the context of this whole that each detailed analysis is justified.

The object of our study, however, is neither to consider the Form-Criticism School for its own sake, nor to investigate any more deeply the differences between Dibelius' works and those of Bultmann, nor even to bring out, for the moment at least, Bultmann's more important conclusions regarding the history of the Synoptic tradition, nor to follow him through all the detail of his analyses. What we feel must be emphasized is the preoccupation Bultmann has for scientific rigorism in all his works, his desire to be scrupulously faithful to the texts. From the time that Dibelius' work appeared in 1919, Bultmann praised it generously, but this did not prevent him from pointing out that the direction of the work, the manner in which its author "constructed" the "forms" before discovering them in the texts, made it susceptible to frequent error. "The first thing necessary is to proceed analytically."

Closely related to his desire for scientific rigor is Bultmann's insistence that research should never sacrifice former acquisitions. In his introduction to the *History of the Synoptic Tradition,* he insists on the legitimacy of analysis which is purely literary, so long as it does not overreach its limits as happened in the works of Wendling, Spitta and W. Haupt. But he adds that "the work of Form-Criticism is not opposed to that of literary criticism." Each is indispensable and presupposes the other. In other words, if Bultmann joined the advocates of dialectical theology as an exegete promoting "Form-Criticism," he distinguishes himself within this new exegetical school which he helped to found by the same exigencies and the same fidelities that distinguished his very personal place among the first friends and collaborators of Karl Barth.

In the same way as his conviction that the exigencies of science and of its problems must be satisfied does not cause him to renounce dialectical theology's fundamental inspiration but rather enables him to give it all the more value, so also his desire for scientific rigor and his preoccupation to respect the previous results of criticism do not cause him to lose sight of the primary objective of the Form-Criticism School: to attain, through the written documents, the living reality which is inscribed in them, the tradition to which they witness. We should not be surprised that five years after the *History of the Synoptic Tradition,* Bultmann published a book entitled *Jesus.*[8] Commentators remarked on the skepticism of the first work, on the "negative appearance" of its conclusions regarding the possibility of learning something about Jesus.[9] One year before publishing *Jesus,* Bultmann published a short work on *Research into the Synoptic Gospels* (1925),[10] in which he wrote: "We cannot define with certitude the extent of Jesus' authentic sayings . . . There is not a single one of Jesus' sayings whose authenticity can be strictly demonstrated." Bultmann's analyses were rightly called "hypercritical," [11] though the word need not be taken in a pejorative sense.

The Form-Criticism School emphasized that previous criticism had come to a dead end precisely because, while hoping to attain an historical nucleus, it had not pushed criticism as far as it could go and had sought this nucleus independently of the forms in which it has been transmitted.[12] At the time that it appeared, the

8 *Jesus* (Tübingen, 1926).

9 Cf. M. Goguel, "Une étude sur la pensée de Jésus" in *R.H.P.R.* (1927), p. 51. We may also consult O. Cullmann, "Les récentes études sur la formation de la tradition évangélique" in *R.H.P.R.* (1925), p. 475; P. Benoit, *Réflexions sur la "formgeschichtliche Schule,"* loc. cit., p. 498.

10 *Die Erforschung der synoptischen Evangelien* (Giessen, 1925).

11 Liechtenhan, cited by O. Cullmann, "Les récentes études . . . ," in *R.H.P.R.* (1925), p. 473.

12 Cf. O. Cullmann: The new school's adversaries "do not recognize that Form-Criticism is perhaps destined to deliver theology from the dead end to which the historicism of the last century brought it" (*op. cit.,* p. 466).

Form-Criticism method was esteemed not only as a considerable advance in the realm of scientific investigation, but also as an invaluable gain on the very planes of theology and religion themselves. To this effect, in his review of the new school's first works, O. Cullmann could write in 1925:

It is strange to see how the so-called liberal critics see a danger precisely where there is the greatest gain. It is true that the new method follows its scientific principle mercilessly right to the end, but in its final conclusions it comes up with a point of view which is essentially religious . . . The Protestant who has experienced the old critical method which was characterized by research for a historical nucleus no longer adores *God in Christ;* he merely tries to adore God *in the same way as* Christ adored him. And this is the only religious bond which still exists between the Protestant and Christ . . . Does modern Protestantism have any way out of this difficulty? Can we return to the Christ of faith without sacrificing scientific sincerity? Perhaps this Form-Criticism method will enable us to escape from our dead end.[13]

As Bultmann would say this dead end results from a poor understanding of history, not only regarding the nature of the documents we use, but also regarding the very way in which we recognize history's significance. The documents never give us merely raw facts; rather, the facts are always expressed in a certain light, and this light is the manner in which the community who witnesses to the facts lived and understood them. As for us, we can perceive the true meaning in these documents to the degree that we are really interested in what they say. Bultmann developed this idea quite precisely in the introduction to his book, *Jesus.* He defines what *considering* his object means. And the first thing he does is to correct his formula. For, he says, the main idea in his book is that "we cannot *consider* history, if we want to comprehend what is essential in it, in the same way as a man considers the world around him in order to orient himself in relation to it." This is true because, whereas a man defined himself by his opposition to nature, he cannot look at history without recognizing that he is part of it and that he himself is involved in the sum of forces which

13 *Ibid.,* pp. 574, 578.

determine its course. When we speak of history, we are talking about ourselves. We cannot look at history from a distance or from outside of it; we can only converse with it in a continual "dialogue." If we try to do the opposite by abstracting ourselves from history in order to approach it disinterestedly, all that we are doing is imposing the subjectivity of our method upon history's condition; we are imposing our point of view—a point of view completely inadequate under the circumstances—and we allow the reality that we are looking for to escape us.[14] To the degree that the categories of objectivity and subjectivity still mean something to us, we can say that it isn't in some kind of illusory "neutrality" that the greatest objectivity can be attained, but rather it can be had only in a personal encounter with history. Instead of imposing external norms onto history, we must receive its message "from within" it. Bultmann tries to bring his reader to this "eminently personal encounter with history," and, to accomplish this, he describes frankly "his" own encounter.

But, we may ask, who is this Jesus whom he encounters, if it is true that we can know practically nothing about him with certitude? Is it an invitation to meet no more than a series of hypotheses? The author tells us that in his book he is "not interested in the *personality* of Jesus." He is persuaded that "we can know nothing more about the life and personality of Jesus, because the Christian sources were not interested in them, and there are no other sources to tell us about him." Nor should we deplore the fact, because a study into the personality of Jesus should only be of secondary interest. If we are interested in a psychological explanation of Jesus' personality, all we would do is apply to this particular case a certain number of laws with which we are already familiar. But Jesus' historical significance, as is the case with any important historical figure, consists precisely in that which is not reducible to these laws and remains unexplainable. What interests us most when we study important historical figures, is not so much their personality as their "work." Nor should "work" be understood as that which expresses or enables us to

[14] A short time before, Bultmann wrote that "in reality, there is no such thing as a neutral exegesis," in *Das Problem einer theologischen Exegese des Neuen Testaments*, Zw. Z. (1925/4), p. 341.

understand their personality, but rather as the result of their existence. And, "for persons like Jesus who acted by means of their
words, what they wanted to express can be reproduced only by
sentences and thoughts, like a teaching." But, he adds, we certainly should not regard this teaching as though it were a statement
of eternal, supra-historical truths. We should rather hear it as the
original message of a man whose words determined the process of
history and whose encounter, if I open myself to it, puts the very
meaning of my existence in question.

Understood in this way, the encounter with Jesus can occur
even if we know nothing about his personality and even if the
documents we have furnish no certain "datum" about his life. All
that is essential, all that interests us, is the message to which
tradition (and particularly its most ancient layer) witnesses and
which, by tradition, is referred to Christ. Even if it is impossible
for us to draw a line between what really comes from Christ himself and what comes from the community, even if the person,
Christ, is only a fiction whose name should be put between quota-
tion marks to designate merely the message in which the Christian
tradition finds its origin (although Bultmann does not think that
this is the case), it would not change anything essential.[15] The
only thing decisive for us is that we should encounter the will
expressed by that voice.

These reflections certainly show us that Bultmann's book, *Jesus,*
contradicts one of the conclusions which he reached in his *History
of the Synoptic Tradition.* He tells us, rather, that he supposes his
former analyses. Far from being opposed in their approach or in
the object they treat, the two works proceed from a common inspiration and complement each other admirably. Without the *History
of the Synoptic Tradition,* the book, *Jesus,* would lack a foundation. Without the book, *Jesus,* the *History of the Synoptic Tradition* would lack some of its meaning. Taken together, they enable
us to comprehend Bultmann's original project, the order of the
questions which he is trying to answer, the direction in which his

[15] We might compare these reflections with those which Bergson made on
the subject of Jesus in *Les deux sources de la morale et de la religion* (Paris,
1932), p. 256.

work is tending, and the method which he has preconceived in order to accomplish it.

The History of Comparative Religions

The Form-Criticism method is an attempt to understand the New Testament texts by situating their place and their meaning in the community whose faith they express. It is used especially to study the Synoptic gospels, in order to determine the history of the tradition to which they witness. However, not all of the New Testament texts are as complicated as the Synoptics, and it is important to clarify the entirety of the tradition, in turn, by situating it in the cultural and religious world in which it developed.[16] This latter work particularly occupies the Comparative-Religions School. *Religionsgeschichtliche Schule* is the name which the theologians who followed in the wake of A. Ritschl's work [17] gave to themselves. By their discoveries in the realm of history and particularly by research into the ancient literatures, they hoped to find new means for understanding Christianity and its origins. The most famous names of the first generation are A. Eichhorn, H. Gunkel, W. Wrede, W. Bousset, J. Weiss, W. Heitmüller, P. Wernle, H. Weinel, and especially the school's theorist, E. Troeltsch.

Bultmann, who had such teachers as W. Heitmüller, H. Gunkel, J. Weiss and others, belongs to the second generation of this school which is still living. His first short work, which appeared in 1910, was a study of *The Style of Pauline Preaching and the Cynico-Stoic Diatribe*.[18] In 1912 he published an important article on "The Religious Element in the Ethical Doctrine of Epictetus

[16] We have already pointed out that Form-Criticism itself profited from this work (cf. *supra*, p. 13). But Form-Criticism came after the work that was done on the history of comparative religions.

[17] And more or less in reaction against him.

[18] *Der Stil der paulinischen Predigt und die kynisch-stoische Diatrib* (*Forschung zur Religion und Literatur des Alten und Neuen Testaments* 13), (Gottingen, 1910).

and the New Testament." [19] In this work, he underlined both the striking analogies which exist between the two doctrines and the profound differences which separate them. Later, he treated of "The Problem of Ethics in Paul," [20] and compared the Pauline ethic with both the Stoic ethic and with Hellenistic mysticism. The following year (1925) he wrote a long article on "The Importance of the Recently Discovered Mandean and Manichean Sources for an Understanding of the Gospel According to John." [21] Here, he utilized the works of Lidzbarski and Reitzenstein, and he advanced a hypothesis by which he sought to clarify the unresolved problem regarding the conditions in which John's gospel was composed. Other studies prepared the larger *Commentary on the Fourth Gospel* which Bultmann published in 1941,[22] in which he gives considerable place to Hellenistic, Gnostic, and Mandean influences. The index at the end of the book can give us a good idea of its orientation; one of the major divisions in this index is devoted to "references regarding the history of religions."

It would be wrong to hold that Bultmann limits comparative studies to John's gospel and to a few Pauline teachings. He believes that our understanding postulates this treatment in all aspects of Christianity. This is the point of view which he supports in his book, *Primitive Christianity in Its Contemporary Setting.*[23] He wrote in the preface to this book:

The origin of Christianity, taken as a historical phenomenon, occurred at the heart of late Judaism which was a product of the Israelic religion described in the Old Testament books and which, itself, was nourished by its heritage. However, primitive Christianity was a complex phenomenon. Its growth and the form which it took were very

[19] "Das religiöse Moment in der ethischen Unterweisung des Epiktet und das Neue Testament" in *Z.N.T.W.* (1912/2), pp. 97ff.; (1912/3), pp. 177ff.
[20] "Das Problem der Ethik bei Paulus," in *Z.N.T.W.* (1924/1-2), pp. 123ff.
[21] "Die Bedeutung der neuerschlossenen mandäischen und manichäischen Quellen für das Verständnis des Johannes-Evangeliums" in *Z.N.T.W.* (1925/1-2), pp. 100ff.
[22] *Das Evangelium des Johannes* (*Kritisch-exegetischer Kommentar über das Neue Testament*, begründet von H.A.W. Meyer), (Göttingen, 1941).
[23] *Das Urchristentum im Rahmen der antiken Religionen* (Zürich, 1949).

soon fostered and determined by the spiritual forces of pagan Hellenism. This Hellenism had conserved the heritage of Greek spiritual history, but it had also been stimulated and enriched by its contact with the religions of the Near East . . . Christianity's proper meaning and its particular character appear when it is seen in relation to the world in which it was born. . . .

But, if he places so much emphasis on explaining primitive Christianity in terms of the religious and cultural world in which it was born, Bultmann never intends that faith should depend directly on the results of this work, or that theology, to the degree that it is centered on the act of faith, can be reduced to this comparative process alone. Theology should remain conscious of the fact that historical science can neither establish nor weaken the "truth" of Christianity, its value as the unique way of salvation. According to Bultmann, theology should look toward an "interpretation" of the phenomena of history which would cause the "possibilities" of human existence to appear. But far from making a personal and supremely responsible decision unnecessary, such an interpretation would solicit it because it would clarify it. And Bultmann already had this perspective when he gave his conference in 1924 on "Liberal Theology and the New Theological Movement." His reproach to liberal theology was that it had not perceived the essentially "relative" character of the results which historical science established. More than once, on the basis of their comparative works, liberal theologians had exalted Christianity's originality and the novelty which it brought into the world. But, Bultmann replied, "novelty is not a specifically divine category," no more than is necessity, which others would like to recognize as the principle of its legitimacy. Whoever would engage in historical research should not forget that God never appears as a "datum" and that we cannot have "direct knowledge" of God any more in history than we can in nature.

In 1926, it was for the sake of these principles that Bultmann criticized M. Dibelius' *History and Supra-historical Religion in Christianity*.[24] And because Dibelius' position is quite nuanced

[24] Bultmann's criticism is reprinted in *G.V.* I, pp. 65ff.

and is not simply identical with that of old liberal theology, Bultmann is led to make some interesting and rather precise statements regarding how he thinks history should be considered in theology. Actually, Dibelius rejects a "naive identification of history with revelation," because he recognizes "that history explored by the historical method is still part of the *world* and that, therefore, God cannot be found in it." This is why he introduces his distinction between the "historical" and the "supra-historical." But, according to Bultmann, this does not enable him to really take Christian faith into account. While he is trying to determine the nature of this "supra-historical" element, Dibelius is invoking a nontemporal, irrational reality, apprehended by some kind of "feeling for values," present as a presentiment in experiences such as love, finding its expression in artistic and cultural symbolism, etc. But this amounts to a replaying of the old romantic themes with nothing new except a phraseology borrowed from the modern philosophies of values. This leads Dibelius to a number of confusions, and he also ends with a serious misunderstanding of the "eschatological" character proper to faith and to the entire aspect of relation to God in Christianity. It is not a matter of considering the historical order and the supra-historical like two "states" which can be juxtaposed. Man's religious life, as is all his existence, is lived in time and in history. For man, eternity can only be a "future." And it belongs properly to faith to open this "future" to man, this "future of God," by freeing him from the perishable past. For this reason, the specific character of faith is not to be sought on the plane of experience or consciousness, but rather on that of action and of decision. On the level of objective, rational observation, there is nothing in Christianity which is, properly speaking, unattainable or entirely of a different order than any other reality of nature. In relation to the exigencies of scientific knowledge, it is a "phenomenon of the world" like any other. But, on the other hand, its "message" is essentially a judgment on the world, a negation of everything which comes from the world. And this double aspect of Christian faith determines theology's task.

This confrontation with M. Dibelius' thought is interesting because it enables us to view Bultmann's position with regard to historico-critical research in general, but especially with regard to the theology common to the Comparative-Religions School. We can note that the themes developed by Dibelius are closely related in more than one way to those we meet, for example, in R. Otto's famous book, *The Sacred*.[25] Bultmann recognized that the attempt which the Comparative-Religions School made to reach the specific character of religious phenomena, while they denounced the insufficiency of rationalistic or moralizing interpretations, was analogous to the original reaction of dialectical theology.[26] He would always class the theologies which developed within the Comparative-Religions School before those which belong to the "old liberal theology" or to the old orthodoxy.[27] Nevertheless, he continually addressed the same reproach to the theologians of the Comparative-Religions School: they were trying to reduce faith to some kind of state or conscious experience instead of seeing it as essentially a practical response to the historical act of God's saving Word.

Once again we see that Bultmann renounces none of science's acquisitions and refuses to place any limits on the purifying work of criticism. He insists that reason should keep all of its sovereignty and that every *sacrificium intellectus* which would "renounce carrying to the very end the rational consideration of history" [28] should be rigorously proscribed. But at the same time as he allows critical reason to work without hindrance in its own domain, he strives to define precisely what the nature of that domain is and he exerts himself to clarify problems by distinguishing the orders. He explains that when we describe religious phenomena by using imprecise romantic concepts, we can give the impression that faith is not a simple phenomenon of the world in which we live. But when we do this, we ourselves remain in this world with its phenomena in which faith can never find the meaning of what is most essential to itself. And there is more danger that the

[25] French translation by A. Jundt, Paris, 1929.
[26] Cf. *G.V.* I, p. 22.
[27] Cf. *Th. N.T.*, pp. 585-86.
[28] *G.V.* I, p. 8.

confusion which results will hide faith's "scandal" than there is that it will manifest it. According to Bultmann, one of Karl Barth's very correct intuitions is his recognition of the fact that liberal theology brought a great blessing when its merciless criticism destroyed all the human supports to our faith and brought us to confide in the only support which it can have: God himself and the saving act of his Word. But he never found himself able to subscribe to the "theological exegesis" which Barth too hastily substituted for criticism.

Throughout his career, his research has been inspired continually by the most rigorous exigencies of the historico-critical method, without ever failing, at the same time, to seek the theological significance of this research. In the lastest of his larger works, the *Theology of the New Testament*,[29] which is both a synthesis of all his research and the expression of his own theology, Bultmann tells us once again that he finds himself, on one hand, "in the traditions of historico-critical research and of the history of religions" and, on the other hand, he bases himself on the principle that the documents "still have something to tell us today." He believes that history and theology have the task of enabling us to hear this message.

The Philosophy of Existence

According to G. Ebeling, the specific difference between Protestant and Catholic theology is that Protestant theology has never been afraid to follow the movement of ideas, has never hesitated to engage itself in the thought of every age, and has opened to humanity these times, in particular, which we call "modern." [30] It is easy to draw a relationship between the Reform and the new spirit of the

---

[29] *Theologie des Neuen Testaments* (Tübingen, 1953). May I also refer the reader to the long review on this important work which I published in *R.S.R.* (1954/3), pp. 434-68.

[30] G. Ebeling, "Die Bedeutung der historisch-kritischen Methode" in *Z. Th. K.* (1950), p. 41.

Renaissance. It is common knowledge that Luther's thought was influenced in a very determined way by Nominalism whose unhealthy work was really the first period in the crisis that was to produce the new world. And, since Protestantism originally was so closely linked to the thought of its times, there is no reason why it should not be able to stay in close relationship with modern thought.

This predisposition, this common origin and heritage of Protestantism and modern thought, is not so much a certain number of axioms or dogmas as a complete opening to and disposition for any spiritual adventure, research or encounter. The only absolute authority which is actually recognized is that of Scripture, or rather that of the Word of God speaking through it. It is true that some will always try to identify the material text with the very Word of God. Most often, however, because a text speaks through the interpretation which we give it, exegesis will tend to become the rule of all theology and even of the life of the Church. Catholic theology has not opposed the findings of science and has generally been quite eager to appropriate them, but it recognizes the precariousness of many of the results. And so its interpretation of Scripture is always carried on "in the Church" [31] according to tradition sanctioned by an authorized magisterium. Although it has its own domain and autonomous methods, it is nonetheless integrated in the whole research of theology, which, in turn, develops within the living faith of the Church. Protestantism, on the contrary, because of its principle, and although it is inspired by different traditions and despite the remarkable sense which it sometimes has for ecclesial values—always tends to return to the fundamental idea that Scripture is interpreted only by itself. It finds itself suspending its faith for the sake of an exegesis whose principle and end

[31] Some Protestants are in considerable agreement with the Catholic point of view regarding the relation between the Bible and the Church. In this respect, E. Kinder reproaches Bultmann because the Bible is not "the book of the Church" for him ("Historische Kritik und Entmythologisierung" in *Zur Entmythologisierung*, p. 38). The New Testament itself, he adds, requires that the Bible be treated in this way (p. 40), and, if the faith of the Church is not our point of departure, other presuppositions will be our points of departure (p. 43). But this reaction is not yet a common viewpoint in Protestantism.

is the exegesis itself. And is this supremely "independent" exegesis not often marked by the particular spirit of the exegete who conducts it? And because he is a man of his times, is it not influenced by the "ideas" which he shares with the age in which he lives?

It is not at all necessary to demonstrate how profoundly Protestant theology understands that, in a certain way, it is going beyond the Enlightenment, Kantianism, Hegelianism, etc. The only difference between modern Protestant theology and all of its past history is that today it willingly admits this influence. It realizes that the different methods which can be used to investigate a reality always correspond to a certain fundamental way of understanding the reality. In other words, it recognizes that every exegesis implies an entire philosophy and an entire theology. But far from being alarmed by this or trying to escape it, it makes it the principle of its reflection and the guarantee of its method. In this way, Protestant theology understands that, in a certain way, it is going beyond the partiality of former attempts because it recognizes the "relativity" of all research and of all reflection. It is this discovery of the fundamental relation which exists between a method and its object, between the questioner and the question, and between the level of reflection and the truth perceived, which constitutes one of the original intuitions of existentialism and of that sense of "historicity" which characterizes contemporary thought, to be resolutely appropriated by a theology like Bultmann's.

It is really modern science which produced philosophy's new way of looking at everything. And we cannot overestimate the importance which the historico-critical method had when it began to be applied to the fields of theology and exegesis. Troeltsch esteemed it enough to say that "the historical method . . . , once it has been applied to biblical studies and to Church history, is a leaven which transforms everything and definitely explodes everything which characterized the older theological methods." [32] According to F. Gogarten, "the original Christian understanding of human existence and of its world in terms of historical existence

[32] *Gesamte Schriften* I, p. 730, cited by F. Gogarten, *Entmythologisierung und Kirche*, p. 16.

was brought into a new light by the modern understanding of history, an understanding which is dominated by the historico-critical method." [33] In the same way, G. Ebeling emphasized that the historico-critical method represents "not only an extreme refinement of the philological method, but also a critical confrontation with tradition, inspired by new intellectual presuppositions." [34]

This method defines a new relation between the believer and the realities to which his faith refers. By a new understanding of these realities, it defines a new understanding of faith itself. Instead of being founded upon a certain number of objects (such as the Bible as verbally inspired, the Church as the "Mystical Body" of Christ, sacraments, etc.) or upon "datums" which transcend human things (such as sacred history counterposed to profane history), faith is confronted with the radical ambiguity of all of historical reality and is affirmed in this ever renewed confrontation. The historico-critical method's concept of faith, as Ebeling remarks, corresponds exactly to the concept of faith implied in the Reform, even if the following centuries did not realize how far it reached. This direct confrontation with the Word of God, beyond any objective security, is just what the principle, *Sola Fide,* demands. All that the Reformation did was to take the historicity of biblical revelation seriously by completely eliminating Docetism.

According to Gogarten, the difference of opinion between Bultmann and his adversaries in their debate over demythologizing, is their radically different concept of history and of all reality with it. He expressed this fundamental point in his *Demythologizing and the Church,* which he wrote to defend Bultmann against the theologians delegated by the Bavarian Lutheran Church to refute him.[35] Gogarten holds that Bultmann's adversaries have retained the Greco-medieval idea of history and historicity, and that they have not understood the revolution which occurred in modern

---

[33] *Entmythologisierung und Kirche,* p. 18.

[34] "Die Bedeutung der historisch-kritischen Methode" in *Z. Th. K.* (1950), p. 27.

[35] E. Ellwein, E. Kinder, W. Künneth, J. Schieder, and G. Merz, whose contributions are collected in *Zur Entmythologisierung, Ein Wort lutherischer Theologie* (Munich, 1952).

times regarding that point of view. Greek thought, and the medieval thought which depended upon it, conceived of history as a series of events occurring in a stable world, so that the science of history was really practiced as though it were outside of history. Modern thought, on the contrary, places the entire world within history, so that history is a final reality and the ultimate problem for speculation. This discovery of the radically historical character of all reality placed man in a new relationship with the world, which is the inverse of his relationship according to the old mode of thought. Today, rather than speak of man as a being in the world, we speak of the "world of man" because man is essentially responsible for the world. When we speak of history today, we always refer to the "historicity of human existence." And this connotes a radically new way of thinking. It means that we have abandoned the fundamental structures of metaphysical thought or of Cartesian rationalism and, particularly, their fatal schema of subject and object. This schema, by which each individualized and isolated the other, always prevented us from perceiving the original relation which constitutes them simultaneously. It is easy to conceive how such a transformation of structures and of fundamental modes of thought should entail a new understanding of all of reality, and, therefore, of faith and theology as well. But Gogarten emphasizes that this new understanding is really only a return to very authentic biblical thought as it existed before Hellenistic metaphysics and its child, rationalism, produced their distortions. The Pauline doctrine on sin, as we find it in Romans 8, 19ff., pictures man as bearing all responsibility for the world and for his history. Our new understanding certainly places man in the center of history. And Gogarten feels that before we renounce this as a modern apostasy, we should ask ourselves whether it is a return to a mode of thought which is remarkably consonant with that of the Bible.

Bultmann, as an exegete, never intended to limit his work to establishing a number of positive "datums" from which a systematic theology could be eventually developed. Had this been the case, he would have been unfaithful to the modern idea of science, of its exigencies, and of its field of competence. His constant concern is to "understand" the realities which are the object of his critical work. And, in understanding them, he wants to analyze them with ever greater penetration. He would be naive to think that the reality could ever reveal itself to us before we begin to investigate it, and that it could reveal itself independently of the question which we formulate by means of our "preunderstanding." Finding the best method to translate and interpret this reality is the major problem encountered, not only by the systematic theologian, but by the exegete and the historian as well, and by anyone who is trying to nourish and guide his faith and that of the Church. According to Bultmann, the most important question for the Church in our times—and perhaps in all times—is a question of theology.[36] It is necessary to find a manner of thought and analysis, conceptual tools, which will enable us to penetrate the realities of faith and express them.[37] And he underlines a deficiency in this regard in many works for which he has otherwise the greatest esteem. He tells us that his work of demythologizing (which we will discuss later in this book) is a question of a manner of thought and expression, a question of language.[38]

A manner of thought and expression is a product of a philosophy. Bultmann remarks that all exegesis and theology are tied to a philosophy to the degree that they have to use a system of concepts. And, because it is fatal to them to be so tied that the philosophy dictates their answers, we must know clearly just what we can refer to and what we can most adequately call upon.[39]

So Bultmann in no way tries to hide the philosophy which inspires him in his exegetical work and his theological reflection and it is the philosophy of existence ("existentialist philosophy"), especially as M. Heidegger formulated it, which he has adopted. He made his choice neither "arbitrarily" nor because of "personal preference," but because this philosophy belongs to the "historical situation" in which his work develops.[40] A product of our age, it

---

[36] Cf. *G.V.* I, p. 84.
[37] Cf. *G.V.* I, p. 75; *K.M.* II, p. 188.
[38] Cf. *K.M.* II, p. 188.
[39] Cf. *K.M.* II, p. 192.
[40] Cf. *K.M.* III, p. 50.

serves the exegete and theologian as well as they can wish. It is not a system that imposes preformed definitive solutions, nor does it require a determined world view. Rather, it reminds man that he himself is responsible for the world and for his own existence, and it merely shows him the general conditions under which he can assume this responsibility.[41] Its main point is that man, as a being, realizes himself in action, in "decision," in the act of his existence.[42] This existence is characterized by "historicity" (or temporality), which underlines the fact that the being of man is identical with a "becoming," a "possibility-to-be," [43] and is distinguished in this way from all other beings in nature.[44] It is within this existence, in the context of this "historicity," that all the problems are found and all the encounters occur.

To the degree that philosophy analyzes the conditions for our knowledge of all human existence, it can help the theologian to consider the particular "possibility" that the encounter with God represents for the human being. It also furnishes a key by which we can understand the final meaning of the documents that are decisive for faith. Far from drawing a screen between the documents and ourselves, it enables us to see through the structures or ways of thought that have not yet been subjected to criticism. Philosophy has no other ambition than to bring us "to the thing itself" to show us its true meaning. And although philosophy itself can certainly never give us the living God, it can put us on the right path to encounter and recognize him.[45] Finally, according to Bultmann as well as to Gogarten, by restoring the meaning of a truly "historical understanding," this philosophy is related to the mode proper to biblical thought.[46]

In its attempt to situate Bultmann in his relation to the various currents in contemporary Protestant thought, this chapter has cited enough affirmations and positions to give us sufficient mate-

[41] Cf. *K.M.* II, p. 192.
[42] Cf. *G.V.* I, pp. 34, 81; *G.V.* II, pp. 8.
[43] Cf. *G.V.* I, p. 118.
[44] Cf. *G.V.* II, p. 243.
[45] Cf. *G.V.* I, pp. 30, 31; *G.V.* II, pp. 8, 228-32; *K.M.* II, p. 187, etc.
[46] Cf. *G.V.* I, p. 323; *G.V.* II, pp. 73, 110, 240, 277, etc.

rial for discussion. However, we will do better to save our discussion for the following chapters where we will examine some of the major themes of Bultmannian theology in greater detail. The preceding pages were intended merely as an introduction to this study. They have undoubtedly convinced us that our project is interesting and that its object requires attention.

CHAPTER TWO

Gospel and Mythology

Karl Barth's work begins with the problem posed by preaching: How are human words able to proclaim the Word of God? Bultmann's however, begins with exegesis in which he tackles the New Testament text and the difficulties we encounter in "hearing" it correctly and "translating" it correctly.

Two Worlds of Thought

The fundamental problem in exegesis is the distance that separates us from the New Testament authors. And we have to overcome this distance if we want to understand the texts correctly. It does not consist merely in the number of years that separate us. Men have changed the world since the time when the New Testament was written. According to Bultmann, the world of New Testament expression is a mythical one into which modern man with his scientific mind is absolutely incapable of entering. Does this mean that the New Testament has nothing more to tell us? How can we understand and interpret it? These are the questions which Bultmann asks.

35

"Myth," he writes, "is the mode of representation in which what is not of this world, the divine, appears like what is of this world, the human. What is above appears like what is below, as, for example, the transcendence of God thought of as spatial distance. It is a mode that represents cult as a material action producing immaterial forces." [1]

Bultmann thinks that it is quite evident that the New Testament's "world image" is a mythical one. And he is satisfied with a simple enumeration to pose the problem that follows from this premise. The world to which the biblical authors continually refer is one that has three levels: our earth is in the middle, heaven is above us, and "the world below" is underneath us. The gods and the angels live in heaven; the "world below" is hell, a place of torment, and earth is not so much the realm of natural events as the place where the opposing supernatural forces meet each other: God and his angels on one hand, and Satan and his demons on the other. These supernatural forces intervene in the course of natural events as well as in man's thought, in his will and in his actions. Miracles are seen as ordinary things. Man is not master of himself, because he can be possessed by demons; Satan can give him bad thoughts, and God can affect his ideas and desires by communicating heavenly visions, by speaking his Word to inspire or console him, and by giving him the natural force of his Spirit. History does not evolve in a continuous or regular course; it moves and receives its direction from supernatural forces. The present age is under the power of Satan, of sin, and of death (regarded precisely as "Powers"). It hastens to its end, a cosmic catastrophe which is soon to occur. The "sufferings" in this end of time, the coming of the celestial Judge, the resurrection of the dead, and judgment for salvation or condemnation, are imminent.

Bultmann adds that a mythical saving-event, "of which the very content of the New Testament message consists," corresponds to this mythological image of the world. According to this message, "when the times were fulfilled," God sent his Son (Gal. 4; Phil. 1, 2ff.; 2 Cor. 8, 9; Jn. 1, 14ff., etc.). This Son, who was divine and preexistent, appeared on earth as a man. Like a sinner (2 Cor. 5,

[1] *K.M.* I, p. 22.

22; Rom. 8, 3), he underwent death on the cross, and in this way he atoned for our sins (Rom. 3, 23–26; 4, 25; 8, 3; 2 Cor. 5, 14. 19; Jn. 1, 29, etc.). His resurrection is the beginning of the cosmic catastrophe by which death, brought into the world by Adam's sin, will be annihilated (1 Cor. 2, 6; Col. 2, 15; Rev. 12, 7ff., etc.). He was raised to heaven and sits at the right hand of God (Acts 1, 6ff.; 2, 33; Rom. 8, 34ff., etc.). He was made "Lord" and "King" (Phil. 2, 9–11; 1 Cor. 15, 25). He will return upon the clouds of heaven to complete his work of salvation, and at that time the resurrection of the dead and judgment will take place. Sin, death, and every suffering, will be annihilated forever. It is soon to occur, because Paul thinks that he himself will witness it. Whoever belongs to the Community of Christ is bound to the Lord by baptism and by the eucharist. So long as he remains faithful, he is assured that the resurrection will bring him salvation (Rom. 5, 12ff.; 1 Cor. 15, 21ff. and 44ff.). Believers already have a foretaste of this life that awaits them, by the Spirit (Rom 8, 23; 2 Cor. 1, 22; 5, 5) who acts in them, who witnesses to their character of sons of God (Rom. 8, 15; Gal. 4, 6), and who guarantees their resurrection (Rom. 8, 11). All of this New Testament mythology refers essentially to Jewish apocalyptic writing and to the Gnostic myth of redemption.

Bultmann continues by saying that it is absolutely impossible for us to take as our own this mythological image of the world, because our mode of thought is that of twentieth-century man who has been "irrevocably formed by science." This does not mean that we are constrained to a narrow scientism that recognizes only what positive science has established. Rather, by means of science, modern thought has been trained to rigor and coherence. On the other hand, mythological thought is characterized by confusion, because it includes in the "order" that defines them phenomena that do not obey the laws of phenomena.

But, remarks Bultmann, the "mythological image of the world" in itself contains nothing that is specifically Christian. It characterizes nothing more than an age in time. What we must ask is "whether the New Testament contains a truth that is independent" of this mythological image and that can still be heard and believed in today. Theology's task, therefore, is to "demythologize" the New Testament.

This task must be correctly understood. "Demythologizing" is only the negative side of an undertaking that is resolutely constructive. Bultmann's critical work on the biblical texts "consists in the interpretation, rather than in the elimination, of mythological expressions"; "it is not a process of subtraction, but a hermeneutical method."

The New Testament's purpose is not to give us a certain "world image." It is trying to give us a message, a living word, that is connected only accidentally with the world of representations in which it has been formulated. No other object than the discovery and expression of this message can occupy the exegete who wants to be faithful to his purpose, to himself, or to all men for whom he is laboring. The most important aspect of Bultmann's hermeneutical project is positive; he wants to establish as precisely as possible the method and the procedure that will enable him to attain this understanding of what the New Testament has to say.

An Existentialist Interpretation

Bultmann's entire hermeneutic is summed up in his work of "existentialist interpretation." And this is the positive, constructive side of demythologizing.

He says that "myth no longer requires a cosmological interpretation; rather, it requires an anthropological one, or, better, an existentialist one . . . In New Testament mythology, we do not need to study the objective content of the representations; instead, our study must concern the understanding of existence which is expressed through these representations." [2] In the propositions that state the Christian message, the only thing which will always retain its value, and therefore the only thing which we should look for, is what they tell us about man and his existence—in other words, what they tell us about the "possibilities" which they recognize for

[2] *K.M.* I, p. 22.

man or which they open to him. This is the fundamental principle of Bultmannian exegesis.

Our first reaction might be to oppose such a deliberate anthropocentricity to which our most basic ideas of revelation and of faith are repugnant. We should point out immediately, therefore, that for Bultmann this reference to existence postulated by all worthwhile exegesis finds its justification and its necessity in God himself. He holds that what characterized dialectical theology is its "considering the historicity of human being" and, more precisely, its considering the historicity of all language referring to God. He thinks that the value of this theology is not so much that it abstracts from man in order to emphasize the transcendence of God, but rather that it never loses sight of man, taken precisely as one who seeks to speak of God in this way and who remains continually under God's judgment. He explains that it makes no sense to speak "about" God, because "at the very moment that we would conceptualize God as an object, he escapes us by that very fact. Our only legitimate idea of God is that he is the almighty, that is, the reality determining all things. Nor is this idea effectively expressed when we speak 'about' God, when we consider God as an object of thought before which we can orient ourselves or take a spectator's impartial point of view by attributing to his reality and essence things that later will have to be rejected or will be accepted if we find the light. A man may have reason to believe in the reality of God, but he should not deceive himself into thinking that he has comprehended something of the reality of God. When we speak 'about' something, we imply that our point of view is exterior to that about which we are speaking. But it is impossible for us to view God from outside of him. And it is just as impossible for us to speak of God by means of universal formulas or propositions, because their truth must always be related to the speaker's concrete, existential situation." [3] And Bultmann remarks that when we speak "about" God in this way, we commit sin as well as error because we are distorting our relation to him.

[3] *G.V.* I, p. 26.

His conclusion is evident: "If we want to speak about God, we have to speak about ourselves." Then we have to state more precisely just what we mean by this. It is clear that we must not confuse almighty God with our own subjectivity. There is no question of listing our experiences or our interior states as if they were immediate manifestations of God's action in us. Indeed, when I turn my thoughts upon the past or project them into the future, I become the object of my considerations. But this "me" refers only to "a phenomenon without existential reality." And "by the very movement of turning on himself to reflect upon himself, the existential subject acts as if he were without God." Our "me" can either be identified with the "objects" of nature or can be defined in opposition to them; it can be integrated with a theistic world view or with a Christian one, etc. However, to the degree that we disassociate ourselves from it in order to judge and dispose of it, it belongs to the order of sin, to the "world" in the biblical sense of the word, that is, to the artificial sphere that we invent in order to escape from both God and ourselves.

Our existence, in fact, is "a thing as singular as God himself. We can no more speak 'about' it than we can speak 'about' him; we can no more dispose of ourselves than we can dispose of him." Regarding this inaccessible existence, "only two facts are clear: first of all, that we must care for it and are responsible for it (in other words, it means: *This concerns you*); secondly, it is completely without security and we ourselves cannot assure it, because to do so would require us to be outside of our own existence and to be God." [4] In other words, we do not leave the inaccessible regions of God, the "completely other," in order to enter the familiar universe of our experiences and ideas; we do it, rather, in order to put ourselves in the midst of the most ineluctable and uncertain of situations and to set ourselves to the most impossible of actions.

If it is true that we can say nothing "about" God or "about" his existence and that any attempt to do so is vain and impious, it is just as true that we are unable to remain silent on the matter. And, by the very fact of choosing to remain silent, we would be taking a position "in relation to" the matter, and so we would end up in the

[4] *Ibid.* p. 33.

same incorrect attitude. Our acceptance of this practical necessity (which should not be confused with a physical determinism), our recognition of the fact that, left alone, all we can do is to reject God and to flee from him and that nevertheless he permits us and at the same time obliges us to proclaim his grace, is what constitutes faith precisely as the continually renewed realization of the humanly impossible. Reference to existence is the condition for religious language, because there can be no truly religious language outside of the act of faith.

Our language, therefore, must be ordered to existence; there is no other way that the New Testament expressions can become the Word of God. But how can we formulate this language? Bultmann remarks that existence sometimes expresses itself immediately, as in the case of simple formulas that convey a human attitude or situation like: "I love you," "I forgive you," "I distrust you," etc. However, existence cannot always be expressed so directly and the meaning of formulas expressing a thought is usually indirect.

Therefore, we need a "science" that will enable us to develop in a rigorous way the "understanding of existence" which all effective existence gives to us. By the very fact, it will provide us with the instrument we need to reach the existential "intention" that seeks to express itself through the different representations in which thought can be projected. This science will be that particular type of philosophy called "existentialist analytics" which serves the function exactly. It will indicate the general, formal structures of what it is to exist humanly, "showing what existence is" and how it manifests itself. And it will furnish us with "the concepts we need to speak adequately of human existence."

Existentialist analytics furnishes us with a screening method that enables us to reach the true and final meaning of the texts. On its results we base our existentialist interpretation which, in turn, calls forth a decision, a commitment, because it restores to the Word its ability to address us. But this interpretation remains in the order of explanation and manifestation. In no way does it force personal decision or substitute itself for it. Rather, it permits us to make this decision in complete lucidity, with full responsibility, basing ourselves only on the decision itself. And precisely in order to grasp the paradoxical aspect of his undertaking, Bultmann stresses that we must understand the distinction, which he considers fundamental, between the two concepts, "existentialist" (*existential*) and "existential" (*existentiel*). He feels that many of the objections made to his work result from the fact that his readers did not grasp sufficiently the radical difference between the two viewpoints to which these words refer.

Whatever we may think of its value, this distinction itself is quite clear. The existentialist (*existential*) order refers to a purely formal or structural viewpoint; the existential (*existentiel*) order refers to the viewpoint of effective, concrete realization. The existentialist viewpoint corresponds to the general structures given in all existence; the existential viewpoint corresponds to the individual form which an existing thing gives concretely, *here and now*, to its existence.

So, when the exegete gives the existentialist interpretation, he is not trying to make his work a profession of faith or of incredulity (because such professions refer, precisely, to the existential order). He is questioning the text and translating it in terms of the universal structures of existence which reflection can establish *a priori* to a certain degree and in which the text can show its meaning. In other words, the existentialist interpretation is an interpretation that considers the *a priori* conditions for the possibility of an exegesis that has meaning for existence, and the meaning for existence is the final meaning.

These "norms" of the existentialist interpretation are not dogmatic or moral imperatives that pressure the will of the inquirer when he is examining the texts or that appropriate to themselves whatever results the interpretation may produce. The norms in question are nothing but norms of understanding. And, rather than hinder, they increase our field of liberty by showing that it is from our liberty alone that our existential conduct proceeds definitively. So, the existentialist analysis of love will establish norms in the sense, and only in the sense, that it will define the general conditions to which all human conduct must correspond if it is inspired by love. But it will not go so far as to tell us "how I should understand my love each time." Instead, "existentialist analysis can only show me that I cannot understand my love each time on the existential plane and that no existentialist analysis can take this personal decision away from me." A rigorous analysis on the plane of understanding, which goes all the way to the final, radical meaning of the texts, and which provokes in this way an existential decision, without, however, imposing its practical direction—according to Bultmann, a decision in the face of the biblical texts which will be a choice between mortal self-sufficiency or faith that opens a future of life—such is the nature of existentialist interpretation.

Man Who Is Challenged

We have to examine the particular philosophical anthropology that Bultmann's work refers to, before we can study any further the particular aspects of a demythologized message whose value comes from existentialist interpretation. What is this man that the philosophy of existence seeks to manifest under its universal forms, this man to whom exegesis must refer if it is to speak a decisive and truly religious language? Bultmann makes striking analogies between contemporary philosophy and the New Testament on the question of what man is in his fundamental traits.

Greek thought saw man as a being of the world, "a part of the great Cosmos, organically incorporated in the objective totality of the universe." Christian thought, however, as well as the philosophies of existence, makes a radical distinction between man and all other beings of nature. That we take into account this radical opposition is the fundamental presupposition of all our understanding of the New Testament message and of the principle of its existentialist interpretation.

Therefore, we have to have a correct understanding of this opposition. It is not the opposition that exists between two contraries in a same species or a same genus. For example, Cartesian and Platonic spiritualisms consider their opposition between the matter of things and man's spirit to be just as fundamental. But their matter and spirit are found in the same world system and, according to Heidegger, in the same category of "beings." The opposition to which we are referring, however, is as radical as we can conceive of, because it occurs in the very order of being. And this is why the being of man and the being of the world, that of the subject and that of the objects in which it "transcends" itself, are always revealed simultaneously. For Heidegger, human being, *Dasein,* consists fundamentally in being-in-the-world. Bultmann emphasizes that in the New Testament the "world" is always the "world of man" constituted by him as it becomes his destiny.

Therefore, man's being is not just one among others, but rather it is being by which and in which being itself is put into question. This essentially "problematic" and uncertain character of human being appears in the fact that it is fundamentally an historical being: "We think that we understand man's existence more correctly (than idealist, romantic, or naturalist thought did) if we characterize it as being an *historical* existence. And when we speak of the *historicity* of human being, we mean that man's being is *possibility-to-be.* That is, man's being is not such that it is simply at his disposal; he is put in question in every concrete situation of life, and he is realized through his decisions in which he chooses *not something for himself,* but himself as his own possibility." [5]

It is in terms of this "historicity" of human being that Bultmann has tried throughout his work to express the Christian faith and the message upon which it bases its decision. This is exactly what he means when he proposes existentialist interpretation. In existentialist interpretation, the findings of contemporary thought bring out more clearly what Bultmann feels he has discovered to be the real meaning in the sources of Christian thought. He believes that one of the most important traits by which Christianity is radically distinct from all other idea- and value-systems of the surrounding world is its recognition and evaluation of time, of "historicity." "According to Christian thought, the essence of 'me' is not spirit in the Greek sense of the word; rather, it is understood as the historically existing 'I' which becomes itself in its concrete decisions in face of what it meets, whether it meets man or destiny." [6] In other words, "for Christians, the temporal character inheres in the nature of man." And even salvation itself never consists in an escape

[5] *G.V.* I, p. 118.
[6] *G.V.* II, pp. 277-78.

from time, as it does for Stoicism or for any kind of mysticism. Christians never think of really meeting God outside of time, but rather of meeting him by converting themselves to it.

That man is a temporal or "historical" being, means that he always realizes himself in an actual decision in which the human subject, by detaching himself from a limited past, confers on it a completely new meaning determined by the future that inspires him. This means that man finds his being only in action whose temporality expresses its necessary structure. Christianity presupposes as its concept of human being that "in act man conquers the true possibility of his being" and that "only in act are we ourselves."

A true act cannot be the result of just any necessity. In other words, although man's being is realized only in act, nevertheless, engaged and manifesting itself in a particular act, it can fall short of its true being. But then it is by reference to this act, and to the authentic being which could conquer it, that every other possibility will be judged. And this will be a path toward nothingness and death from then on.

The will is the organ of action. Since man's being is realized in act, it is easy to understand that "his real essence is not the *logos,* reason or spirit," but that it is instead the will. So for Christianity —which agrees on every point with contemporary thought— "human existence, life understood precisely as human, must always be considered as a tension, a desiring, a wanting."

It is important to note, however, that when Bultmann refers to the will, he is not talking about a kind of "faculty" which rules the options and superficial conduct of the soul according to anterior dispositions or according to a transcendent Good which reason perceives by reasoning on the absolute. "Man is not master of his will in the sense that, due to his *logos* or reason, he might detach himself from it or overcome and guide it by means of his rational thought"; that, rather, is the Greek concept. For Christianity, "man himself is his own will." This will is expressed in the fundamental act of liberty by which the entire being of man puts itself in question in order to realize itself in a "decision" that completely qualifies it.

The Division Made by Faith

Within this general, structural understanding of human existence and human being, the New Testament speaks a particular Word. This Word divides existence, and the division is that of faith. The two resulting parts of the division are the two fundamental types of existence: "existence without faith" and "existence under faith." The first is characterized by the "care" that sets man to look for his security and to base it upon visible things that are at his disposition. This security is only illusory. It really hands him over to defeat and death. Daily experience proves the fact. In his desire to base his security on worldly objects, man enters into conflict with other men who are seeking the same objects for their own security, and he must either fight or compromise with them. From this arise envy, anger and quarreling, along with contracts and conventions that may reestablish some equilibrium though it will always be fragile and necessarily provisory. There results an "atmosphere" which smothers a person at the same time as he contributes to cause it. In reality, a slavery to agony and fear weighs on man. Each one cramps himself and his own welfare with "the secret feeling that everything escapes him, even his own life."

In opposition to this, there is existence under faith, which is an existence based upon the invisible over which man has no power. It is an existence which, by the very fact, renounces all security produced by human industry. Such a life becomes "possible" for man only by faith in God's "grace," by trusting that he will encounter the invisible, the unknown, in the form of a love which will open a future to him and that this, precisely, is life itself.

God's grace forgives sin. This means that it frees man from the past which enchained him. Sin is the attitude which exactly defines existence without faith. Sin is a closing of oneself against the invisible, against the future where God awaits man to give himself to him. Faith, on the contrary, is the opening of oneself to this future, in freedom. At the same time, it is always an "obedience" and implies that man must renounce himself and all security and all will to establish his own worth and to make his own life. Faith is the decision not to trust in self, but rather to trust entirely in God "who raises the dead" (2 Cor. 1, 9) and "calls to existence that which does not yet exist" (Rom. 4, 17). It is the march of liberty that wrests us from the world and from everything that attaches us to it.

This detachment from the world that specifies faith has nothing in common with ascetical effort. Rather, it is an "aloofness from the world" by which we are in the world without being of the world. Actually, the believer exercises his sovereignty over everything (1 Cor. 3, 21–23). He is free to do anything (as the Gnostics say), but without letting anything have power over him (1 Cor. 6, 12; cf. 10, 23ff.). He can rejoice with those who are happy and weep with those who are sad (Rom. 12, 15), but he falls no longer to any worldly ambition (1 Cor. 7, 17–24). He looks upon every reality in this world as not having importance in itself, and he retains a complete indifference (cf. Phil. 4, 12; 1 Cor. 9, 19–23). To him the world is crucified, as he himself is crucified to the world. The power of new life that animates him works without weakness in suffering and in death, because, precisely in recognizing his nothingness, he can receive from God everything he is and everything he has (2 Cor. 5, 12ff.; 6, 8–10).

The Christ Event

However, according to the New Testament, faith is not a possibility given to man connaturally with his existence. It is a possibility opened to us by an event, the event which is Christ.

It is true, Bultmann remarks, that faith is not a "mysterious, supranatural quality," but the living of an authentically human existence. In the same way, love is not a "mysterious, supranatural behavior, but the natural comportment of man." However, the question we must ask is "whether man, taken as he exists effectively, is natural man, if he disposes his "nature" so freely."

According to both the New Testament and philosophy, man can never become but what he is (cf. 1 Cor. 6, 11; 5, 7; Gal. 5, 25, etc.). But the New Testament holds that in order to become what he is, man must first of all be returned to himself. His fallenness is such that without the salvific action of God, any movement he makes is a movement of fallen man. Recognition of this fallen state, particularly by philosophy, far from remedying the situation, can only increase it, because the pretension of escaping it increases his fatal self-sufficiency and pride.

In this way, Christian faith, in its principle, is faith in sin and in the liberation from sin. But isn't this a mythological element? The answer depends on a free decision: the commitment of faith. Outside of faith, man remains blind to sin and does not see his culpable self-sufficiency; any doctrine about sin necessarily seems mythological to him. In faith, on the contrary, where he grasps the fact that his entire existence is suspended from the gratuity of divine love, he understands that the only possibility for him to find his true life is for him to be freed from himself and from the self-sufficiency which cuts him off from that love. And the very reason for the New Testament is the announcement of this liberation: "It affirms that there where man cannot act, God has acted for him." This, precisely, is the meaning of the Christ event on which the work of demythologization and existentialist interpretation must concentrate.

Bultmann remarks that in the New Testament text "the historical and the mythological (concerning Christ) are mixed in a unique way," with evident contradictions. However, the mythological elements have no other reason than to express the "meaning" and the "scope" of the history of Jesus in the eschatological work of salvation. In this way, the references to his preexistence and the virgin birth exist only to show that the importance of the person of Jesus for me should not be measured by what appears in historical, objective observation, and that it is vain to look for it on that level. These texts about Jesus have no other purpose than to say that "the question of his historical origin need not be asked, and that his true significance will begin to appear only when we no longer occupy ourselves with such questions."

But what about "the basic question regarding the cross and the resurrection" in which, quite evidently, all of Christian kerygma is concentrated?

According to Bultmann, the New Testament introduces a certain number of mythological elements (the crucifixion of the pre-existent Son of God who became man, a sacrifice whose blood expiates our sins, etc.) in order to account for the event that happened on Calvary. But these elements have no other purpose than to bring out the cosmic dimensions of the event and to express its historical and eschatological consequences. To the degree that these dimensions are understood in faith, the cross is an ever present event "for us." And, in fact, the cross becomes a reality present in the sacraments (cf. Rom. 6, 3. 6; 1 Cor. 11, 26; 10, 16) and in the concrete unfolding of the believer's life (cf. Gal. 5, 24; 6, 13; Phil. 3, 10).

How can we perceive today the true meaning of the historical fact of the cross? To answer this question, Bultmann distinguishes between the disciples' situation and ours. Because of their direct, personal bond with Jesus, the cross was for the disciples an event of their own life and, in this way, manifested its meaning. But the crucified Jesus is by no means proclaimed in the New Testament as if the meaning of the cross were to be revealed by his life as history would eventually picture it. "He is proclaimed as the crucified who is at the same time the resurrected." The cross and the resurrection cannot be separated. In their reality as a "cosmic" event they are only one.

According to Bultmann, what the New Testament tells us about the resurrection has no other purpose than to express the meaning and the consequences of the event on Calvary. The resurrection was not destined to be a miracle provoking or encouraging faith. The elements in the New Testament which would lead us to believe that this is the case were added later (Acts 17, 31; Lk. 24, 39–43; the empty tomb narrations, etc.). Paul doesn't know about them. Rather, because the resurrection is essentially "an eschatological event," it is itself presented as an object of faith. And faith in the resurrection is nothing else than faith in the cross as a saving event, as the cross of Christ. The cross "is not an event of salvation because it is the cross of Christ, but it is the cross of Christ because it is an event of salvation. Outside of this, it is the tragic end of a generous man." [7]

[7] *K.M.* I, p. 46.

How can we come to believe in the cross as a saving event? For Bultmann, there is only one possible answer: "Because it is proclaimed to us as such." We are not to ask for proof that the preaching which comes to us as the Word of God is legitimate. It is merely a matter of believing. However, this faith is not a blind, arbitrary decision, because at the same time it opens to us the possibility of understanding ourselves. Our yes or no is therefore "an intelligent yes or no."

"Intelligent faith in the Word that is preached is the authentic paschal faith." The paschal event, as an event which historical science sees at the side of the cross, is "nothing other than the birth of faith in the resurrected, in which preaching finds its origin." The historian can account for this birth "up to a certain point" by reflecting on the bond between the disciples and Jesus. But paschal faith is not interested in a question of historical science. "Paschal faith's birth is a fact studied by history; but for paschal faith, as for the first disciples, the manifestation of the resurrected man signifies God's act in which the saving event of the cross is accomplished." It is this act that constitutes the object of faith. Like the faith of the disciples that is its origin and like the Church where it continues to resound, it is this act which the word of preaching concerns and which belongs to the eschatological event of salvation.[8]

By placing the entire content of the New Testament message in this eschatological intervention of God, Bultmann thinks that he has eliminated all the mythological leftovers. He thinks that he has answered the true intention of the New Testament by emphasizing and giving value to its fundamental paradox. Contrary to myth which tends to confuse the divine and the human realities by making the divine appear immediately in the human, the eschatological schema, as Bultmann understands it, maintains an extreme tension between them and identifies them only paradoxically. And it is to this paradox, this "scandal," that faith refers. Faced with the world and with science's image of the world, faith's attitude is defined by its "however" (or the "as if . . . not" of 1 Cor. 7, 29–31). Not the myth, but eschatological faith justifies the affirmation: "The Word was made flesh."

[8] *Ibid.* p. 47.

Critical Reflections

Bultmann's project of demythologizing and existentialist interpretation, as well as his formulation of the Christian message that results from it, has divided the theological world into three camps: (1) his enthusiastic followers who discovered in this "new theology" a solution to all problems, (2) his bitter adversaries who see his work as the ruin of faith and as a disguised rationalism which they hoped had ended, (3) his moderate followers who recognize in his program a justified concern, but who reject the radicalism with which he defined it and realized it effectively.

We are naturally quite tempted to support this last position. Before adopting it, however, we should remember that Bultmann himself has said that compromise is impossible and even "absurd." "Is it not precisely concerning the New Testament's central affirmations that the problem begins to burn?" He tells us that demythologizing is not a matter of sorting out what problems to eliminate and what ones to keep.

In other words, in Bultmann's opinion, any criticism of his undertaking is inadequate if it concerns only his practical application or its degree of radicalism. Actually, his project forms a whole in which all the elements are conditions for each other. Even if we recognize the seriousness of the preoccupations which command the system and the correctness of some of the intuitions which inspire it, we cannot in face of it outline a reaction to the whole.

We immediately see how legitimate it is to want to express a Christianity which speaks to man and in which the essentials of the message are not obliterated by a multiplicity of formulas or misunderstood representations. By his observations on myth and its fallacious identifications, as well as by his insistence on the "eschatological" character of faith and on the "scandal" attached to recognition of the salvation brought by Christ, Bultmann indirectly, but very correctly, recalls the divine transcendence and the fact that all relation to God must necessarily come through the cross. When the Church denounced Monophysitism centuries ago, it seems it was combating the same confusion—that is unjustifiable to reason and ruinous to faith—which Bultmann also has pursued on every level.

The effort toward understanding and criticism which he wants to develop within the most fundamental religious approaches represents in itself a healthy and undoubtedly necessary thing if these approaches are to retain their correctness and purity. We cannot help but agree with him when, regarding the Amsterdam profession of faith, he remarks that everything has not yet been said, that serious ambiguities still remain after we have confessed Jesus Christ, not only as Savior but even as God, and that we must always ask ourselves what we mean.

Then too, we cannot deny that Bultmann has found some very attractive formulas to describe the *attitude* of faith. He helps us to rediscover the stupendous actuality in some of the Pauline or Johannine themes. His theology is undeniably rich in *spirituality*. And Christian preaching finds in his work more than one principle of renewal.

However, the "kerygmatic concentration" which he confers on this preaching and the narrowly "practical" character of the spirituality he proposes, cannot fail to provoke a feeling of stiffness and monotony. In spite of what he intends or says, Bultmann's instrument in New Testament work does not allow him to respect the value of all its revelation. When he does disengage a significant theme in preaching or spirituality, his conceptual instruments are much too rigid to base a true theology on it.

We already see this rigidity in his position regarding demythologizing. No one can deny that the interpretation of the New Testament is a problem and that its representative elements are not always immediately evident to men who are living in an entirely different cultural context. We must make an effort to translate it if we want to understand correctly what the Word intends to reveal. And Bultmann has progressed beyond any simplism which would equate myth with fable. He recognizes that myth has a positive meaning and that it must, therefore, be interpreted rather than eliminated. However, the very general meaning which he advocates for it does not allow him to explore all of the power to reveal which contemporary philosophy and anthropology have discovered in myth (or in what he describes as myth though it often pertains, rather, to symbolic language in general).

Mircéa Eliade has written: "Today we are beginning to understand something which the nineteenth century could not even foresee: namely, that symbol, myth and image belong to the substance of spiritual life, and that we can disguise them, mutilate them, or degrade them, but we can never extirpate them. . . . Myths are degraded and symbols are secularized, but they never disappear, though it be the nineteenth century, the most positivistic of civilizations. Symbols and myths are too ancient: they are part of the human being. And it is impossible not to find them in any existential situation of man in the Cosmos." [9]

In fact, never before has there been so much interest in the study of myth as there is today. Nor is this an interest to denounce illusions and to affirm our triumph over a way of thinking, feeling or living that has ended. Rather, it is an interest in studies which bring out the riches and the stupendous power to reveal that fill myth—so that only an impenitent rationalism could neglect them. M. Eliade writes further that "the power and mission of Images is to express everything that will not submit to concept."

We should also reflect on Paul Ricoeur's interpretation of symbolic function. He writes that it belongs to our age, after having critically "emptied" language, to be able "to fill it again." Having passed "through the desert of criticism," today we feel the need of being "challenged" again. And this, precisely, is the inalienable function of symbols and myths. They "give us something to think about." [10]

Bultmann's incapacity to account satisfactorily for the inalienable function of symbol is naturally connected to his narrow concept of existence.

In his borrowings from Heidegger's philosophy, he spends most of his time retaining a number of distinctions, but he neglects everything that this philosophy can tell us about the "poetic" sense of mystery. In order to talk about this, Heidegger, while always remaining in the realm of philosophy, used symbolic language ever increasingly. If there is anyone who does not seem to feel the need to "demythologize" for the sake of rigor, it is he. Bultmann is

[9] *Images et Symboles* (Paris, 1952), pp. 12, 31.
[10] Cf. "Herméneutique des symboles et réflexion philosophique" in *Il problema della demitizzazione* (Rome, 1961), pp. 51ff.

fascinated as much by a fear that the mind will lose itself in its representations, as he is by his eagerness to spare man a *sacrificium intellectus* which he thinks has nothing in common with true faith. Actually, his very fear (terror!) of objectifying thought (can one be sure that another thought exists?), which guides Bultmann, shows that he really is still bound by it and that instead of having gone beyond it, he has willingly accepted its laws and remains closed in the artificial dilemmas it engenders. Bultmann is still prisoner of an idealism which is powerless to contact the substance of things.

We discover this idealism in the fact that his theology is incapable of giving meaning to the body when it describes existence in faith. The realities in which the body evidently comes into play (as, for example, in work or in the sacramental gesture) are given no value of their own. Bultmann's writings mention work only to denounce the exaggerated value it is given by contemporary civilization. As for sacrament, he recognizes it as nothing more than a *verbum visibile* in which the "visible" aspect brings no more to the Word than a supplementary danger of hiding or perverting it. Still more fundamentally, he distrusts the doctrine of the "body" of Christ; he thinks that it gives evidence of the Gnostic influences that weigh upon the New Testament.

This ignorance of the proper meaning of the body necessarily goes along with his forgetfulness of the meaning that nature holds more generally in the spiritual becoming of man. Bultmann's explanation of the "existence" of this spiritual becoming is not sufficient; it is not merely a burst of pure liberty, or the "event" of meeting a voice, or a "neighbor" whose "challenge" puts me in a state of being able to "decide." It also plays a role at the very heart of a certain number of fundamental relations which I certainly have to assume and, up to a certain point, form, but from which I can never abstract myself. They always precede and envelop the movement of my liberty: relations of generation, of filiation, of consummation, etc. We often hear mention of the "acosmism" of Bultmann's theology. The term is exact. In the same way, Bultmann, who is always talking about history and historicity, actually removes all the meaning of real history and leaves only an emaciated "decision" which I make in an instant (and which expresses precisely what he calls my historicity). "A philosophy of history whose task is to decipher the hidden sense" of this history, is, according to him, destined to fail and makes no sense at all. The only thing that merits consideration is that point-in-time, the instant, of an existence which escapes from the opacity of time and nature. Properly speaking, nothing but that instant exists.

A Marxist would immediately call such a thought "bourgeois idealism." Whatever we may think of the habitual oversimplifications in such judgments, we wouldn't reject it in this case, for we would perhaps recognize that it is a lesser evil! However, we feel that we can search further for the meaning of such a theology and can try by the very fact to sketch the direction research should take to surmount its insufficiencies.

It is certainly evident in Bultmann's theology that it belongs to an historical movement which outlined itself first of all and fundamentally as a break with tradition (which it considered suspect and perverted) in order to return to an immediate contact (in reality, an abstract one) with the Word of God contained in Scripture. In a more general sense, it also considered itself a break with the Church in its actual unity as in its historical continuity in order to encounter the God of justice and mercy directly without the risk that he be veiled by his intermediaries. This religious movement, the Reform, occurred within a still greater upheaval: the dislocation of Christian society, of the *Corpus christianum*. In every domain the same desire for emancipation manifested itself. This effort for liberation tended to absorb the greater part of the intellectual and spiritual energies of those who supported it. The Reform presented itself as a "protest" against the established ecclesial "order" and the theology reigning at the time, and as the absolute negation of what should have been handed down. Later, the French Revolution would consecrate the negation of a social order which had been sacrosanct up to that time, in order to substitute a reign of abstract principles of reason for it.

Today we are becoming increasingly conscious of the abstraction in this new order, on the political and social plane (for example, criticism of "formal democracy") as well as on the religious plane. Interest in the reality of tradition, of the Church and of sacramental symbolism, considered to be of prime importance nearly everywhere today, is one of the signs of this new awakening. It corresponds to a preoccupation with recuperating realities that were lost sight of during the course of previous centuries due, according to the different "parties," to the impassioned desire for evangelical purity, to a dogmatic stiffening or to the intemperate development of critical reason. As we said above, the rediscovery of the value of images, symbols and "myths," is one of the important aspects of this modern movement. It occurs within an immense effort undertaken today to restore to man and to his intelligence their true stature in the world and in history. The reevaluation of the imagination, which guarantees the bond between understanding and sensitivity, between thought and body, will allow us to rediscover the value of the "images" through which divine revelation is given to us. They refer us to him who is "the image of the invisible God" (Col. 1, 15).

Anyone who wants to pass over these images or to try to extract a meaning from them which could subsist without them, and which maintains no real organic ties with the images themselves, not only wants to escape the human condition but also is trying to step outside of the economy of salvation as well. If there is an historical revelation, and if salvation has actually been manifested and realized in the world, this revelation and salvation will always be communicated to us in the world of images. And these images are reality itself because they have been formed by the Spirit of God.

Does this mean that we can remain content with literal repetition of the biblical formulas? Don't we need to consider the exigencies that modern criticism has deepened and the difficulties our contemporaries have when they try to understand ancient religious language, difficulties which are again confirmed by the great interest people have shown in Bultmann's work? We would only be abstracting ourselves once again from our historical condition if we ignore the new demands that critical consciousness has brought to bear with ever greater intensity. We would be taking this biblical language full of reality and be degrading it to a collection of formulas, either magic or related to a pure, non-temporal intellectuality. If, contrary to what Bultmann says, the world in which we live and think is continuous with the world of the apostles and the first Christians, and if our faith should let itself be formed and nourished by the same fundamental images because these images contain in themselves all reality, then the only way that we can really let that world contact us, that we can benefit from the power to reveal in these images and the transforming strength of this reality, will be to approach them with the exigencies we have as twentieth-century men. We must scrutinize their permanent and inexhaustible actuality at the end of this evolution which has made us what we are. In other words, it would be illusory and empty to try to recover an ingenuousness forever lost. But, if we must accept the demands of criticism without subterfuge, we must always remain capable of situating it in its place. We know that we have the right, and that we are in a position not to let it devour us, because it is a grace given to our age that we understand not only the undeniable exigencies of reason but also the relativity which constitutes its function.

In order to make ourselves accessible to the power to reveal in the language of the ancient religious texts and monuments, we must first discover the course of their meaning through history in the tradition that they created. This task imposes itself at least on those who intend to communicate the Bible's authentic message to the men of our time. And they must not attempt to do this by means of questionable criteria borrowed from a narrow concept of existence, "demythologizing." Instead, by means of theological work based on history, they must grasp again the discourse of faith inaugurated by the incarnation of the Word of God. Careful not to break it, they must never more fear to continue it.

CHAPTER THREE

The Word of God and History[*]

Contrary to liberal theology which tended to reduce Christianity to a phenomenon of consciousness or of history, dialectical theology was the reaction of a faith centered on the divine Word of revelation. This Word is entirely gratuitous and transcends every reality of this world. Since the very beginning of his work, Bultmann has taken part in this return to a theology of the Word of God in the spirit of the Reformers: the Word attested to in the Bible and ever again provoking the believer's decision.[1]

He brought to this theological renewal his original efforts as a New Testament exegete. By means of his exegetical work, he came to recognize that only an authentic theology of the Word could provide the end in which his research would find its definitive meaning. His minute analyses of the sacred text, and in particular his patient study of the Synoptic tradition, brought him to consider the New Testament writings to be living witnesses of faith. And this, in turn, led him to emphasize their essentially kerygmatic character. This is why the new work in "Form-Criticism," to

[*] This chapter appeared in the collective work, "La Parole de Dieu en Jésus-Christ," in *Caheirs de l'actualité religieuse* 15 (Paris, 1961).

[1] Cf. on this subject, H. Bouillard, "Genèse et évolution de la théologie dialectique" in *Karl Barth* I (Paris 1957).

which Bultmann made an eminent contribution, was greeted so enthusiastically by Oscar Cullmann, who thought that it would finally enable criticism to escape from the "dead end" to which the last century had brought theology and, with it, an important part of the Protestant Church.[2]

From the numerous "datums" of the New Testament writings considered to be problematic or even legendary, liberal theology hoped to extract a "nucleus" of historically certain truth upon which Christianity might continue to construct itself. Bultmann, whose entire formation took place within liberal theology, always retained his critical skepticism. But at the same time he was not afraid to criticize the erroneous perspectives that affected all of its research. He feels that we cannot circumscribe the historical nucleus with either precision or certitude. He stresses, especially, that for faith and theology it can have only a relative interest anyway. Any project to "objectively" reconstruct the past proceeds from an illusion concerning the very nature of history, because history can never be "considered" objectively, from a distance, in the way that we abstractly consider the phenomena of nature. This is because we ourselves are part of history, we ourselves are involved in the system of forces that defines its course. We can only regard these forces as solicitations, original invitations addressed to our liberty. It is only in this way that historical research can find its true meaning. It is only in this way that we can begin to speak about the Christian faith and theology.

What is true of history in general, is particularly true of the men who shaped its course. However, the important thing about them is not their "personality" but their "work": the action in which they engaged themselves and as a consequence of which the world was changed. And in a world of men where a real action is measured less in terms of the physical energy it takes than in terms of its shock on minds and hearts, the "work" that most often interests us is the one that is accomplished by word. This is at least true for him on whom Christian faith recognizes its entire dependence and for whom theology must account as its primary object: Jesus. When we study Christian origins, what we should definitively look

[2] Cf. *supra*, p. 18.

for is not to know the "personality" of Jesus nor the "datums" regarding his life, most of which are very problematic. Rather, we have to try to understand the message which the different traditions of primitive Christianity refer completely to the manifestation of Jesus Christ.

In the book which he published in 1926 entitled *Jesus* [3], Bultmann tried to retranslate this message in its stupendous actuality and to make heard again the voice which should remain living for us even though we can no longer see the face of the man who spoke it. He devotes a good amount of his theological work to establishing that this way of seeing Jesus does not proceed only from a necessity imposed by criticism or from general reflections on historical consciousness, but that it corresponds primarily to the Christology we find in the New Testament. Bultmann tried to demonstrate this at a congress of Swiss theologians who had asked him to explain what he, as a New Testament scholar, thought of the Christological confession of the Ecumenical Council of Amsterdam which recognized Jesus Christ as God and Savior. After he had pointed out the ambiguities in this formula and had shown that the New Testament declarations about Jesus are always soteriological, even functional, Bultmann turned to what he considers to be the most exact and significant category, the one that furnishes the essential theme in John's gospel. If we must confess Jesus Christ as God and Savior, it is only—but very really—insofar as he is the *Word* by means of which God addressed us to save us and to give us life. [4]

Two Concepts of the Word

Bultmann's theology, therefore, can be considered a theology of the Word of God. It wants to develop a faith that adheres to the Word by means of which God reveals himself to us in Jesus Christ. He feels that it is essential to his task that he state precisely the nature of this Word. And in studying his pursuit, we will be able to

[3] Cf. *supra*, pp. 17-18.
[4] Cf. *G.V.* II, pp. 246ff. Cf. *supra*, pp. 51-52.

determine many aspects of his theology. We will contact the element which is its very heart and which defines its whole orientation.

In order to understand the nature of this Word from which, according to Bultmann, all of Christian faith is suspended, we must keep in mind a distinction he considers fundamental. When I hear a word, it can evoke within me the thought of a reality that was known long ago or the "remembrance" of a truth whose principle already lived in me before I ever formulated it. For example, Socrates pointed out that Menon, his slave who was without any education, already knew mathematical propositions before anyone taught them to him and all that was necessary was that he be helped to reach them.

This purely evocative function of a word confers only a transitory value upon it and leaves it a stranger to intelligible content which could subsist without it. But along with its evocative function, a word has another in which it reveals itself as actually creating the reality which it proclaims. Isn't this true, for example, of such simple words as, "I love you," "I hate you," "I forgive you," etc., which define an essentially contingent historical relation? This is what gives to certain words their disturbing power and often a seriousness that is irreparable. A word of injury or a simple word that expresses a sigh of love brings something new into the world of two persons, and it can change the entire course of their lives.[5]

Bultmann invites us to take a look at how these two ways of regarding the Word have existed historically in Hellenism and in the Bible.

Hellenism primarily considered the meaning or content of the Word (the *logos*). What is proper to the *logos* is that it brings an intelligible reality to light, or rather that it unveils itself in this reality that it constitutes. It subsists in itself, independently of him who thinks it or pronounces it. A man has only to find in each individual reality he beholds the universal *logos* which founds it and in which he himself participates. And this *logos* that founds all existence and all reality does not need to be pronounced by a living voice in order to be discovered. It is not "heard," but "seen." It is

[5] Cf. *G.V.* I, p. 157.

true that speculative thought, as well as foreign influences like the mystery religions, during the course of centuries transformed the concept that the first Greek philosophers had. Early Greek thought saw God and the world, being and thought, as one fundamental unity. This was still the case for the Stoics, who added only the idea of an essential dynamism in virtue of which the *logos* could, for example, be identified with the *pneuma* that animates nature and gives rise to it in its different elements. Later, a fundamental dualism [6] which radically opposed two substances—the one divine, simple and eternal, the other terrestrial, mixed and perishable—was substituted for the monism of primitive times and of Stoicism. Then, in order to continue its function of making the world intelligible, the *logos* tended to become an intermediary who transmits the power or the thought of an inaccessible God. In this sense, he became either the creator or the ordering principle of the world, or the revealer, the "envoy," the "son" of God. However, although he is related to a divinity from which he emanates, a divinity who speaks to him in order that the world may find its meaning and man may attain his salvation, he is never the living Word who challenges, whose contingent event upheaves a situation and releases a movement of history. It is never the very appearance which is important. Rather, the thing considered is his intelligible or marvelous content, the mysterious wisdom which he unveils and proposes. The only reason why he must be spoken like a word is that this wisdom is not itself within man's power, but must be received from an inaccessible source. And when man appropriates this wisdom or word, it is no longer identified with the divinity. Rather, it bursts out of a mysterious "silence." And it is toward this silence that man, through the mediation of the *logos,* must direct himself in order to find his true being.[7]

Quite contrary to this is the concept of the Word that dominates all of the Bible, despite its numerous nuances and incontestable evolution. For the Bible, the Word of God is first of all and fundamentally a manifestation of his power. The primary and deter-

---

[6] Replacing the simple distinction between matter and form which, one way or another, was always necessary.

[7] Cf. *G.V.* I, pp. 274-79.

mining factor of the Word is not its intelligible content, but the
fact that it was pronounced. It is not the subsistent and eternal
truth which it expresses, but the event which it represents from the
moment that God pronounces it. This is why the Word is not only
judgment (in logic's meaning of the term), but challenge, com-
mandment, judicial sentence, etc. It always concerns man definitively, that is, a freedom which can hear it and conform to it.
Even when the Word of God determines natural events and presides
over the workings of the world, it doesn't find its meaning and
subsistence in itself like a system of eternal laws. It continually
proclaims to man that there is a very personal relation between the
creator and his creature which the latter must recognize in a practical way. This same Word expresses itself really in the events of
the world and of nature on one hand, and on the other hand in the
human words by which God, through his prophets, expresses his
efficacious will to men. And this is in no way an emanation or a
reflection of an eternal order of justice. Rather, it is the manifestation of a personal will whose reasons are fathomless. But this
Word that expresses a power that is beyond man's strength is also
the one that reveals to him his true situation and gives to him his
true being. Outside of it, all authentic reality is radically closed to
him, especially that of God. It is useless to look for God independently of his Word. Better still, we can say that for us the Word of
God is nothing else than God himself, a God on whom we turn our
backs as soon as we try to find him in contemplation, in *théôria*, a
God whom we can never encounter except in the act of his revelation if we listen to him and obey him.[8]

Challenge and Event

It is, of course, within the framework of biblical tradition as
continued by late Judaism that the New Testament expresses its
doctrine of the Word, rather than in the framework of Hellenism.
Jesus presents himself as a person commissioned to proclaim the
decisive Word of God by announcing the coming of his eschatolog-

[8] Cf. *G.V.* I, pp. 268-74.

ical kingdom. He doesn't bring a new doctrine about God, a new wisdom, or a new world vision. Rather, he brings a call to penance, to conversion, to final decision. By the very fact that he presents himself, he demands that man take sides in face of the definitive manifestation of God's will which is expressed by his voice. "Nothing he says is new, but the decisive thing is the time, the *now* of the declaration, the very event of the Word." Faced by him, the important thing for man is not that he penetrate more deeply into the understanding of divine mysteries, but that he "hear" the call and "do" the will which it expresses.[9]

After the death and resurrection of Jesus, the Word of God becomes identified with the Christian kerygma, but it always retains its same characteristics. It is an efficacious word of authority; its meaning and importance cannot be distinguished from the act, the event, of its proclamation. It is a word that demands to be heard and effectively followed.

The Christian message always presents itself as an existential call ordered to a practical response in the person addressed. But it also "communicates" something, an "historical fact," the "event" which is named Christ. It is an essentially "actual" message, but it is also linked to an historical tradition whose origin occurred within the history of the world, in a determined point of space and time, which enters the competence of historical positive science. This problem regarding the actuality of the Word of God accomplished in Jesus Christ and its link with history and with tradition is one which occupies Bultmann very much. He feels that its solution is necessary for a correct understanding of the Christian faith.[10]

According to Bultmann, this faith is the taking of a very determined position with regard to the Old Testament, and it defines itself as such. He has often underlined the importance which the Old Testament had for the primitive Christian community as its holy book. He has listed some of the problems which this causes. And he shows that, because of this, primitive Christianity could not help but take note of its own proper situation and its newness.

9 *Ibid.*, pp. 273-74.
10 Cf. *G.V.* I, pp. 279-93, 153-87; *Th.N.T.*, pp. 464-73.

A theology of the Word of God merely translates a certain understanding of Scripture which itself proceeds from a particular way of looking at the relationship between the two Testaments. This relation is the one between the eschatological accomplishment and its temporal preparation. And it expresses, also, the link between history and revelation, which, according to Bultmann, is the important question in all theology of the Word of God and of the Christian message.[11]

He tells us that "the relation to history is a constitutive characteristic of the Word of God in the Old Testament." [12] This Word was always a manifestation of power; it formulated an exigency; it showed a path, and proclaimed a promise. It always concerned the present moment. But it supposed, first of all, the history of the People of God in whose midst it burst forth. By recalling past events, it gave Israel its faith and hope and assured the continuity of future progress. And one of the essential characteristics of successive times was its compromise with the history of the people. In this way its link with human history was quite different from the one which characterizes the New Testament. In the Old Testament, the Word of God unfolds itself through the succession of times, "at diverse times and in many ways," as the Epistle to the Hebrews says, by means of many messengers, which correspond to the prolonged course that the People of God had to follow in order to reach the end that was assigned to them. In the New Testament, however, the Word of God is unique and is identified with him who is the Word itself and who will not be remembered in the way that Abraham, Moses and David are remembered, but who will never be anything else than the very act of the preaching that announces him.[13]

We should not let this aspect draw us off the track, and we must mention immediately another aspect which will enable us to understand what, according to Bultmann, the Word of God is essen-

[11] Chapter IV is specifically concerned with the question of the Old Testament in Bultmann's theology.
[12] *G.V.* I, p. 287.
[13] Cf. *ibid.*, p. 332.

tially. Though it manifests itself in many ways, the Word of God in the Old Testament is rigorously one to the degree that it is the Word of the same God founding and directing the same history. In reality, it is one to the degree that it reveals a foundation within history which should characterize the end of history—to the degree, in other words, that it already announces Jesus Christ. Inversely, the new light of the New Testament, which announces the accomplishment of this salvation, continues to shine down through the ages of world history; it is carried by a multitude of preachers and gives rise to a new People of God that assures its transmission precisely through the infinite number of points in time and space.

The Word of God contained in Scripture is never the Word because of what it says: because of the objective content in its sayings. Even in the Old Testament, where the history of the chosen people constitutes the most constant theme, this history does not become Word of God except in the ever renewed act of prophetical preaching which refers it to the eschatological intervention of God who will bring all history to an end. And for us who are no longer within the motion of that history, the Old Testament cannot in itself be the Word of God.[14] Even for the Jews, it existed only at the final point in a movement of hope which brought them beyond their terrestrial history. And this is what gives such importance to their experience of failure, manifested in the exile, the dispersion, etc., which was to bring them to despair of all conceivable salvation. In other words, the Word of God is really the Word of God for Israel only in its inaccessible terminus. It is, properly speaking, the Word of God only in God himself, and his relation with history was one of power and effectiveness rather than one of consciousness. The relation of consciousness always took second place. It is expressed in the prophets' disturbing words and in the obscure faith of humble people. In Bultmann's theology, the Old Testament never represents the road that God patiently followed in order to reveal himself; it is never the condescending conversation that he held with his people in order to let them penetrate progressively into the mystery of his being and his plans.

---

[14] Cf. *ibid.*, p. 333.

It is nothing else than the human echo of his salvific will. In
its objective form, it can never be considered his Word but
"indirectly."

The New Testament is no different in this regard. We have
already noted that the importance of Jesus' preaching was not so
much what he said as the event which this preaching represented.
In the same way, the narration of what he lived, suffered and
taught does not constitute the message. Rather, the event and the
very fact of its proclamation constitute it. Its content is merely
the simple *fact* of God's historical intervention which is given in the
preaching of the Church, and the Church finds its origin in the historical manifestation of Jesus Christ. In the Old Testament, the
link between prophetical revelation and history consists simply in
the fact that this preaching proceeds from a given historical situation. But it is the Word of God for the obscure hope of those it
disconcerted, standing beyond everything which the prophet could
say or conceive of. In the same way, the link between the New
Testament message and history consists entirely in the fact that
this message must be preached *here and now* and that this preaching, itself contingent, supposes *as its point of departure* what
Bultmann calls the Christ event. But the purity of the message is
found only when history is completely reabsorbed into eschatology [15], that is, beyond everything it can say, into the very act which
transcends all history and all consciousness, by which God justifies
me in spite of my sin. The Word of God is first of all and essentially this act of efficacious power and sovereign freedom.

The divine intervention occurs in our history. And this Word,
whose reality exhausts itself in the very act of its proclamation, is
pronounced through human words that enable it to echo through
the consciousnesses of men and to leave behind its historical
effects in our world. "If the Word of God does not arise from any
human criterion, if it is an authoritative word, it is just as true—
since it is precisely because of this—that it is an *intelligible* word.
It doesn't act by means of magic force, and it doesn't demand
blind submission like a dogma does, or an acceptance of the ab-

[15] Cf. "History and Eschatology" in *New Testament Studies* I (1954), p.
11.

surd. If it were not intelligible, it would not be a word-addressed-to-someone." [16] This is why Christian kerygma, though it transcends every doctrine and every teaching, always formulates itself within the framework of a theology whose problems and categories it borrows. It does this because it has to contact individual men who express their life and their "understanding of existence" by means of these problems and categories. This is also why, inversely, it cannot be permanently fixed in any of the formulas it has borrowed down through history; it must be able to reach men whose essentially temporal existence never ceases to transform itself.[17]

Although we see that the Word of God expresses itself by means of the words and systems of human thoughts, we must never forget that it cannot have more than an "indirect" identification with any of them. This identification is always the fruit of an eschatological act that can neither accomplish nor prepare any progress in our natural understanding. In the encounter between the divine freedom and the human freedom which is operated by faith, the element of consciousness and understanding, as necessary as it is, always takes a second place. Like Moses on the mountain, we never discover God until he has already passed. Bultmann insists, when he comments on the discourses after the Last Supper, that Jesus himself is always, for the believer, he who "is continually about to take his leave." [18] The *Logos* is truly the light who enlightens the existence of men,[19] but only *on the basis of* the radical upheaval which he once worked, and no human path can ever lead us to progress toward this light.

Critical Reflections

These theses on the Word of God involve all of Bultmann's theology. He certainly appreciates the transcendence of the divine Word and God's sovereign freedom that is expressed in it and that

[16] Cf. *G.V.* I, p. 282.
[17] Cf. *Th.N.T.*, pp. 580-81; *G.V.* I, pp. 180ff.; *Ev. Joh.*, p. 432.
[18] *Ev. Joh.*, pp. 432, 486-87.
[19] Cf. *ibid.*, pp. 31-32.

even gives us the faith by which we recognize it. This is one essential aspect of the Word of God which he brings out remarkably, one which makes the faith of Israel and that of Christianity irreducible to any other religious experience.

It is surprising that after having made such extensive use of the history of religions to analyze the influences that the New Testament authors experienced, he uses only a narrowly Judaic vein that doesn't even comprise the whole of biblical heritage to define the Christian message. He doesn't take the sapiential tradition into account, although it existed alongside of the prophetical tradition without contradicting it. Indeed, the sapiential elements in the Old Testament complement the prophetical and enrich them with new perspectives. On the other hand, Hellenistic Judaism certainly borrowed from its cultural milieu. And its borrowings were not necessarily perversions or compromise, but they contributed to the broadening that was a providential preparation for the New Testament. As authentically biblical as they are, the works that are collected in the New Testament are all written in the Greek language. The Old Testament text to which they generally refer is that of the Greek *Septuagint*. How can we think that we can express ourselves spontaneously in any language without taking not only some of its modes of thought, but also the intellectual and spiritual experiences to which this language witnesses?

Bultmann labors to show us that John's gospel, for example, formulates a message that is diametrically opposed to that of Gnosticism, even though it expresses itself, to a degree, within the conceptual system of Gnostic mythology. Without doubt, the revelation which John transmits to us is absolutely original, and has nothing either equivalent or analogous to any other ancient religion or speculative system. Today no one takes seriously Renan's identification of the Johannine *Logos* with Philo's *Logos*. But does this mean that John was not trying to answer, or at least to relate to, the ancient problems in its regard when he used the term? It was, after all, the world to which his message was addressed. At least one exegesis that we should not too quickly forget, that of P. Rousselot and J. Huby, interpreted this as the reason for John's use of the term *Logos* in his prologue to the fourth gospel.[20] Today, C. H. Dodd thinks that "Johannine Christianity" cannot be understood except against the background of rabbinical Judaism, Hellenism and Hellenistic Judaism (represented by Philo). Without detracting from St. John's essential originality, he nevertheless emphasizes that his gospel "certainly presupposes many ideas that correspond remarkably with those of Philo," and that the Johannine doctrine of the incarnation of the Logos, and it alone, can fully satisfy the "elements of personal piety, of faith and love, which are found in Philo's religion, but are not integrated into his philosophy. . . ." [21]

There is something quite analogous to this in the influence that Greek thought had on St. Paul.[22] However, Bultmann is far from ignoring the Gnostic, Stoic, and other influences, which the New Testament authors felt. So we are not reproaching him for that. Rather, his adversaries usually accuse him of giving them too much importance and say that in doing so he is following an outmoded criticism. What we object to is the radical break he makes, on the one hand, between the act of the divine Word and, on the other hand, the formulas in which it is given natural expression and intelligible content. He makes this break so neatly that he can find a pure and very narrow Judaic prophetism in a New Testament that is impregnated with Hellenism, and he says that there is only a purely "eschatological" identity between the content of the Word of God and this Word itself. In other words, according to Bultmann, the words of the Bible are only mere human words in their "direct" immediate meaning. They become God's words only in the act of a preaching that puts my existence into question. And it is proper to this preaching to restore before me a call whose existential meaning has no necessary link with the

[20] Cf. *Christus* (Paris, 1912), pp. 740-42. J. Starcky maintains that St. John uses the term *Logos* in his prologue "more with reference to the Hellenistic *Logos* than to the biblical *Dabar*" ("Logos" in *Dictionnaire de la Bible. Supplément,* col. 495).

[21] Cf. in this regard, D. Mollat's review in *R.S.R.* (1956), p. 424.

[22] Cf., for example, H. Schlier, *Die Zeit der Kirche* (Fribourg, 1956), p. 165, n. 9.

sacred text except that of a pure *that* whose origin is simply one of fact. The Word of God can never be objectified in any other way; and this "facticity" itself is possible only because it can be entirely assumed into the purely "eschatological" act of the Church's preaching and the existential decision of faith.

We have already tried to show that this concept of the Word of God does not correspond to everything that Holy Scripture tells us. It neglects an essential aspect of the Word, one which, it is true, was especially developed by Greek thought, but which, as we said above, is not absolutely lacking in the Bible.

The Word is never merely an inert instrument that communicates to us the determination of a foreign will, or that we must serve in order to express our own sentiments or our own will. It is within the Word that we already begin to feel, to think and to want. Language and words, as has been correctly remarked, "form men much as they are formed by men. . . ." They constitute a "world," a certain "order of existence," within which every individual is born and moves. "From the depths of our most intimate me, we live in the Word and are formed by it." [23] We can inflect the meaning of words addressed to us; we can give them a particular bent, infuse a new power into them, and enrich the common treasure of language with an original creation. It is no less true that these novelties ground themselves in an environment of exchange and communication within a social system of meaning, within a certain language.

The Word of God, a manifestation of his power, is itself inconceivable outside of this world of meaning upon which it bases itself at the same time as it creates it. The sacred authors and the centuries of Christians who followed them always understood the Bible as the "Word" of God in the most complete sense of the term. At the same time as it is the personal witness shaking our existences, the Word of God was always understood as the place where two consciousnesses encounter: the *organ* of a divine revelation which enlightens the understanding *at the same time as* it converts the will. The Word of God, as it is contained in the Bible and continually echoed in the Church, at the same time as it is

[23] R. Guardini, *Das Gebet des Herrn,* 7th edition (Mainz, 1954), pp. 37-39.

the saving *act* of the *living God,* also presents itself as the *conversation* which the *God of truth* held and continues to hold with men whom he wants to find in all their humanity in order to transform them into himself.

It seems to us that this understanding of the Word is already implied in the use which the New Testament makes of the Old and in the interpretation which it gives to it. Not only is the Old Testament considered to be the announcement and preparation for the definitive revelation brought by Jesus Christ, but it is essentially in its light and language that the New Testament expresses itself. In order to really transform hearts, the Gospel had to penetrate intelligences; and it could not have been the full and definitive revelation of the Word of God in any other way.

The way that Bultmann depreciates the importance of the Old Testament is characteristic of both his exegesis and his theological elaborations. He does this because he is suspicious of any idea of a development or pedagogy within revelation. He thinks that such a perspective is proper to Hellenism.[24] It is rather paradoxical, but nevertheless true, that a too Semitic idea of revelation causes him to minimize the Old Testament revelation. He cannot bring himself to admit that the Word of God might really be identified with the phenomenon of consciousness and history, or at least, according to him, this identification cannot be made strictly except in the "eschatological" act of faith. It can have no reality outside of this act which itself can have no basis outside of itself. This explains his position with regard to the problem of Jesus' messianic consciousness. He does not hide his conviction that Jesus did not know that he was the Messiah, and he says that the question, which belongs only to historical research, is without theological importance.[25] But isn't it precisely in the consciousness of Jesus that there occurred in its fullness the identification between the Word of God as witness to his thought and will, on the one hand, and the faithful and perfect echo of a human consciousness, on the other? Isn't it in the mystery of this consciousness that the meaning of the many words which make up the Old Testament was under-

[24] Cf., for example, *G.V.* II, p. 69.
[25] Cf. *Th.N.T.,* pp. 25-33.

stood in its fullness? But this is the mystery which was revealed to the disciples, beginning with Jesus' mortal life and becoming achieved after he had suffered and entered into glory, and which they, in turn, have announced to us. The Word of God is not formulated for us merely *about* the coming of Jesus, and it is not merely *about* this coming and the preaching which we continue to hear even in our own day, as is the case in Bultmann's theology. Rather, it is given substantially in his theandric presence and subsists in the mystery of his body that died and rose from the dead.

The thing which rules Bultmann's theology of the Word is evidently his fear of seeing revelation, and therefore all our relation with God, made into some kind of substance. Any admission that a purely prophetic presence passed over into an incarnate presence is repugnant to him. The question we can ask ourselves in this regard is whether theology—to the degree that it wants to remain integrally faithful to Scripture itself—should not manifest a certain reserve toward a New Testament exegesis and a doctrine of the Word carried too far, in the same way as often happens in our day when a too exclusive value is placed upon the Semitic structures of revelation. By showing us where exact but too unilateral positions usually take us (and this by means of the rigor with which he develops the consequences of a well-defined position right to the end), Bultmann may help us to formulate our own faith more correctly.

CHAPTER FOUR

The Role of the Old Testament In Christian Faith*

We have already seen that the existence of the Old Testament, and the value which was given to it, is what contributed most to primitive Christianity's definition of its faith.[1] As an exegete and theologian of the New Testament, Bultmann understands his task to be one of giving direct account for this faith. He has never studied the Old Testament for its own sake. But he has had to indicate, at least, what a Christian can look for and find in it. He returns to the question in many chapters of his work. And he does this to the point that we can find a characteristic orientation of his theology in it.[2]

* This chapter appeared in the *Nouvelle Revue Théologique* (1956).

[1] Cf. *supra*, pp. 65-66. *Th.N.T.*, pp. 94ff., 107ff.

[2] Besides the passages from the *Theologie des Neuen Testaments* which we have cited, also consult: "Die Bedeutung des Alten Testaments für den christlichen Glauben" in *G.V.* I, pp. 313-39; "Christus des Gesetzes Ende" in *G.V.* II, pp. 32-58; "Wiessagung und Erfüllung" in *G.V.* II, pp. 162-86; "Ursprung und Sinn der Typologie als hermeneutischer Methode" in *Th.L.* (1950), col., 205-12; "History and Eschatology in the New Testament" in *N.T. Studies* (1954), pp. 5-16.

Inadmissible or Insufficient Positions

In his attempt to determine what the Christian faith can and should find in the Old Testament, Bultmann begins by eliminating several kinds of considerations which he feels are either inadmissible in themselves or lacking in theological meaning.

He tells us that it is quite evident that the Old Testament can be seen from a different point of view than that of faith. For example, the historian can look at it as a witness to one or more stages in the development of ideas or religious experiences. This viewpoint is in itself legitimate, so long as it does not take itself to be more than it is: a positive study which leaves the final and properly theological meaning of its results dangling. So long as we hold to it, we are continually abstracting from the specific and fundamental affirmation of Christian faith, namely, that all relation to God is connected with the person of Jesus and that there is no true religion outside of him. And to the degree that the historian's viewpoint is considered to be the final, definitive one, it necessarily implies a relativistic vision of the historical "datums." And this is nothing but a refusal of faith.[3]

Consideration of the Old Testament from the viewpoint of historical development is not the only one that cannot be held as properly Christian and believing. There are other ways of looking at it and treating it which the historico-critical method has rendered "impossible." [4] Such is the attempt to study it as *a book of prophecies*. "On one hand, the prophetical pretensions of the Old Testament are not prophecies at all; on the other hand, they refer neither to Jesus nor to the Christian community. They contain merely the Israelite and Jewish image of the future they hoped for." [5] We can be sure that the Old Testament prophets did not look forward to the same events as those which we have afterward assigned to be the fulfillment of their prophecies. Furthermore, when we draw out one of these appropriated prophecies, most of the texts have to be turned in a way contrary to their primitive meaning. This, for

[3] Cf. *G.V.* I, pp. 313-17.
[4] Cf. *G.V.* II, p. 165; I, p. 335.
[5] *G.V.* I, p. 335.

instance, is why we go to the Septuagint text rather than to the Hebrew test. If we tried to use the Hebrew text, most of our learned transpositions couldn't even get off the ground.[6]

Alongside of this work of falsification that is imposed onto the original texts, there is another mode of procedure borrowed from Hellenistic culture which enables the interpretation of the Old Testament as a book of prophecies to develop almost without limit: this is the *allegorical method*. It allows us not only to extract from the whole Bible a certain number of determinate oracles, but it is a means by which the entirety of the Old Testament can be regarded as prophetical of what was realized in the New Testament. Bultmann recognizes that typology, moralizing interpretation, etc., can be distinguished from allegory in the strict sense of the word. On occasion he has distinguished between the mechanisms proper to each of these different forms, adding, however, that they are often found combined and contaminating each other.[7] But the only important point, or at least the only one that interests us, is that all these procedures (whose use is not specifically Christian) are not invulnerable to criticism. Bultmann feels that these methods always deliver the texts over to an arbitrary exegesis and that they always tend toward fantasy and childishness.[8] The most they can do is let us say in a new way what we have already known in another way. We can expect no original truth from them.[9]

Some of the more modern attempts at interpreting the Old Testament in its relation to Jesus Christ are more enticing. Such, for example, is the nineteenth-century one developed by J. C. Hofmann in his book, *Weissagung und Erfüllung*. According to Hofmann, it is neither the words of the Old Testament as such, nor every specific detail of its content, which have truly prophetical value; rather, it is the *dynamism of the history* which the Old Testament passes on to us. Israel's history is prophetic to the degree that it is a movement toward an end and continually con-

[6] Cf. *G.V.* II, p. 165.
[7] Cf. especially the article previously cited: "Ursprung und Sinn der Typologie als hermeneutischer Methode." Regarding the distinction between typology and allegory in general, also cf. again: *Th.N.T.*, pp. 115-16.
[8] "Jede Allegorese ist Spielerei oder Unfug" in *G.V.* I, p. 335.
[9] *Ibid.* Cf. again *G.V.* II, p. 168.

tains this end within itself. History can be regarded as prophetical only if we are standing at the point of its accomplishment. Only then does it manifest the meaning and end of its movement precisely. For Hofmann, Christ is the actual meaning and end of Israel's history, and with it, of the history of the world which can be seen extending prophetically toward him.[10]

Bultmann remarks, however, that we must ask just what theological meaning such a viewpoint can have. It certainly doesn't serve to establish the importance of Christ, since it itself is based on this. And if we object that his importance arises precisely from the fact that we can base all of world history on him, we are supposing that a religious truth can be propped up by philosophy of history. But such an idea betrays a basic misunderstanding of the transcendence of faith and of the realities it involves. In fact, "according to the New Testament, Christ is the terminus of salvation history, not in the sense that he represents an end toward which an historical development directed itself, but because he is the eschatological end." [11]

A final way of looking at the Old Testament is more than legitimate. It opens to us an understanding which, in a way, cannot be surpassed. It consists in looking for the manifestation of a *fundamental possibility of human existence* and of the understanding which we can have of this existence. Like every historical document, the Old Testament can be summed up as a call: a challenge addressed to us.[12] And this is so much the more true, because our past was formed especially by biblical tradition and Greek humanism. These two elements determined the situation which was the point of departure in the realization of our freedom.[13] More precisely, biblical tradition helped to waken us to the understanding of historical existence without which we could not attain a true understanding of faith. And in this regard, the content of the Old Testament is perfectly consonant with what we find in the New. They both show us that time (history) constitutes the very being of man and that his ideal is not a contemplation or *théôria* of the

[10] Cf. *G.V.* II, pp. 168-70.
[11] *Ibid.*, pp. 170-71.
[12] Cf. *G.V.* I, p. 318.
[13] Cf. *G.V.* I, pp. 322, 332.

divine nature, but rather that it is the attention given to the Word of God and to the exigencies which it manifests to us in the instant. The Old Testament, like the New, sees no other relation with God than one of faith, and this relation of faith is one of practical fidelity, obedience, trust, etc.[14]

But does this last viewpoint account for what was proper to the Old Testament in its determination of the Christian faith? Does its meaning, differing only in content, remain in the same order as Platonic philosophy or all the manifestations of Greek humanism? And if the understanding of existence is fundamentally the same in the Old Testament as it is in the New, what is essentially new about the New Testament? So long as these questions remain unanswered, we have not determined what the Old Testament means to Christian faith.

Law and Gospel

Bultmann writes that "during those ages that still maintained a truly historical relation with the Old Testament, the understanding of existence expressed in it was opposed to the Christian understanding by the antithesis of *Law and Gospel*." So when Bultmann tries to answer this question precisely—the question, namely, of how the Old Testament can and must be regarded for Christian faith—he refers to a tradition that goes back to St. Paul, but which was later marked with Luther's strong influence.[15] However, in this point as in every other, his thought remains nevertheless very personal.

He says that if we want to correctly understand the opposition that exists between the Law and the Gospel (and this opposition must serve as principle for a Christian interpretation of the Old Testament), we must determine just what the Law means, because the Old Testament identifies itself with the Law. The Law does not consist merely in the totality of ordinances which express the will of God for the believing Jew. If, for the Christian, the

14 *Ibid.*, pp. 323-24.
15 *G.V.* I, p. 319.

Gospel has taken the place of the Law, and if Christ is the "end" of the Law, then we are still in a time of divine commands and such a notion has not been superseded. Faith itself is "obedience," and he who lives it should not "put the body's parts at sin's disposal as implements for doing wrong. . . , but rather put them at God's disposal as implements for doing right" (Rom. 6, 13). Faith does not deliver us from the Law as though it were an insufferable burden. And Bultmann remarks in this regard that we must not interpret St. Paul in the same way that Luther did. For Paul, as for all the Jews, the Law was never a real burden, and it is not as such that he shakes it.[16]

Neither does Paul make any distinction (nor should we) within the Law between one part which has been surpassed (directives referring to cult and ritual, for example) and another part which still retains its value and remains in vigor (the purely moral prescriptions referring to the interior exigencies of conscience).[17] The opposition between the Law and the Gospel does not regard content. Rather, St. Paul attacks a fundamental attitude by which man places his confidence in the Law to give him some kind of value (worthiness) in God's sight. What the New Testament and the faith it expresses contest is the idea that "the accomplishment of the Law is a way to salvation." The Christian message, the Gospel particularly as Paul proclaims it, is a message of salvation, of "justice," which is obtained by faith alone, and salvation is a gratuitous gift of God.

Therefore, Law and Gospel express two fundamental ways of

[16] Cf. *G.V.* II, pp. 32-33.

[17] It is true that this distinction is possible. Alongside of the positive ordinances and connected with the historical and sociological context in which they were formulated, Bultmann remarks that we find in the Old Testament the expression of essential moral exigencies that correspond to the nature of the human condition as such, and, in particular, to its fundamental characteristic of existence-in-common. These latter exigencies certainly remain valid in every time and every place. For this reason, however, they have no intrinsic connection with the Old Testament, even if the Old Testament can, in fact, enable us to perceive them more clearly (cf. *G.V.* I, p. 320). In any case, what we must comprehend well, Bultmann tells us, is that Paul's reflections on the Law do not concern this distinction, and that "his fundamental attack against the Jewish Law is of an entirely different kind than Jesus' attack" (cf. *G.V.* II, pp. 36-37).

being, two forms of existence. When we oppose them, we are looking at a twofold possibility or, we might call it, a double principle of life: either a life guided by the concern to avail oneself of one's own strength or, instead, a life conscious of its own fundamental powerlessness and nothingness which waits for the pardon and grace of God.[18]

These two ways of existence condition each other, and it is impossible to develop an understanding of the one without developing an understanding of the other. In fact, it is only the man who has experienced his own powerlessness who can experience grace. Still more, he must continually renew this experience, because grace, far from being something we possess, is rather the ever renewed forgiveness for the ever renewed movement by which we constitute ourselves sinners.[19]

So, the Gospel message cannot be understood except by someone who has also equally understood what the Law is. Does this mean that a person must live under the Old Testament in order to be able to understand it? Doesn't the Law manifest itself in other ways? Bultmann thinks that the answer to this is quite evident. When Paul is speaking to the pagans to teach them about the Gospel message and trying to convince them of their powerlessness and sin, he never needs to call on the Old Testament for help. "He knows that the pagans, who do not have the Law, nevertheless know by nature what the Law commands; their consciences witness to the fact that the word of the Law is written in their hearts." In other words, the Gospel requires a preliminary understanding of the Law, but this understanding can be obtained either from the Old Testament or from other realities in which the divine Law manifests itself. "Everywhere man has been given the possibility of coming to know his nothingness and of humbling and despairing of himself; everywhere he also has the temptation to make of this moral obligation a means for obtaining his own justice and to think that by struggling, by works, by self-education, etc., he can make a moral personality for himself and attain his authentic being, or at least that he can and should attain it. Everywhere

---

[18] Cf. *G.V.* II, pp. 37-43.
[19] Cf. *G.V.* I, pp. 319-20.

there can develop that zeal for God which Paul calls an ill-informed zeal (Rom. 10, 2) and which, precisely, encounters the message of the cross." [20]

The Church still uses the Old Testament in its preaching, but for purely *pedagogical reasons*. And in these perspectives, it has good reason to do so. Nowhere else does the meaning of moral exigencies, of the responsibility of man before other men and before God, of the importance of the actual practical decision, etc., manifest itself so vigorously and clearly.[21] And we have already considered how important the Old Testament was in constituting the past that formed us. We have seen that we must continually recall this past if we want to know clearly the possibilities of existence which we have to assume and if we want to realize fully the historical existence outside of which we cannot speak of Christian faith. But none of this suffices to make the Old Testament a unique type of document, a holy book, or the immediate expression of God's very Word.

The Jew and the Christian

The preceding reflections all depended on the identification which we made at the very beginning between the Old Testament and the Law. However, is this reduction legitimate, and is the relation of the Old Testament to the New expressed adequately by the opposition between the Law and the Gospel? We said that existence under the Law and existence under grace mutually suppose each other. The Gospel is not possible for anyone who does not know the reign of the Law in one way or another. It seems that we can also say, on the other hand, that a man can see what the Law truly is, only by means of the true light which delivers from the Law. Doesn't the experience of the Law in the Old Testament itself require a certain experience of what the grace of the Gospel is?

Bultmann recognizes that the Old Testament is far from being

[20] Cf. *G.V.* I, p. 321.
[21] Cf. *ibid*.

ignorant of what grace is. The gift of the Law itself appears as a grace. Still more, Israel knows that it does not owe its existence to its obedience to this Law, but rather that it owes it to the gratuity of divine choice. And it knows that if it could continue to exist despite its innumerable infidelities, it is only because of the ever renewed forgiveness of a God who is just as merciful as he is just. Even though we can note considerable differences between the various books and authors of the Old Testament, we still find a good many passages that give undeniable witness to a truly ontological understanding of sin and of the divine forgiveness which, alone, can deliver from sin.[22] Above all, in its tragic history and in its impossible conviction that God's act should be identified with the destiny of its people, the Jewish soul spontaneously projected itself in an act of foolish hope right to the end of times. In other words, the Jewish soul could anticipate what Christian faith now considers to be already realized.[23] We can also say that "from its own viewpoint, the Old Testament is both Law and Gospel." [24]

But it can no longer be such for us. The history of Israel is no longer our history, and we can no longer base on it our faith in the eschatological intervention of the saving God.[25] On the contrary, it is proper to Christian faith that in Jesus Christ it has recognized this eschatological intervention which, as such, has ended any idea of identifying religious history with the history of a people. In fact, this eschatological intervention should not be likened to the interventions by which, according to the Old Testament, Yahweh chose Abraham, delivered his people from slavery in Egypt, directed their march through the desert, etc. This eschatological intervention is not a continuation of these "datums" in the history of Israel; rather, in a strict sense, it marks their end. Our faith is not nourished by recalling it, in the way that the Jews could nourish theirs by recalling the gift of the Law on Sinai, their passage

---

22 Cf. *G.V.* I, pp. 326-30.

23 Cf. *G.V.* I, pp. 330-31. Cf. again *G.V.* II, pp. 171-83, where Bultmann treats this point with greater precision by describing the development of the ideas of alliance, kingdom and People of God.

24 *G.V.* I, p. 333.

25 Cf. *G.V.* I, pp. 322, 333.

through the Red Sea, their entrance into the Promised Land, etc. Its actuality is not expressed in the continuity of the history of a people, nor in the tradition which hands down and assures this continuity. "The message of forgiveness conferred in Jesus Christ by the grace of God is not the historical narration of a past event, but the word of the Church's preaching which now addresses itself immediately to each of us as the Word of God and in which Jesus Christ is present precisely as the Word." [26]

For this reason, we cannot find God's revelation *directly* in the Old Testament, in the history it relates, or in the experiences it describes.[27] The Old Testament can no longer enable us to hear the living Word of God's grace. It can help us to reach a more profound *idea* of God's mercy and forgiveness, as it can of our nothingness. However, in itself it is no more necessary for this purpose than it is for the purpose of enabling us to know our radical need and our sin.[28] In any case, it can in no way be identified with the Gospel of grace which absolutely marks its end.

The "Mediate" Character of the Word in the Old Testament

Isn't there any way in which we can recognize in the Old Testament the very expression of the Word of God and, according to the traditional way of looking at it, the prophetic announcement of what the Gospel proclaims? The Old Testament is certainly considered prophetic by anyone who recognizes the internal contradic-

[26] Cf. *ibid.* I, pp. 331-32.

[27] Cf. *ibid.* I, pp. 333-35.

[28] Bultmann remarks that also outside of the biblical sphere, we meet the idea of the nothingness of man, who is a fool when he pretends to measure himself against the divine power to whose mercy (grace) he is completely subjected. It is true that the attitude that proceeds from this fundamental intuition is not the same in Hellenism (measure, modesty, etc.) as it is in the Bible (trust). Bultmann notes this difference (*G.V.* II, p. 52), but he does not draw out all the conclusions that it suggests. Doesn't the Old Testament present itself as the revelation, and not only a natural revelation, of a God whost love must be spoken before we can rest in it?

tion which it bears from one end to the other, or better, the radical failure which this contradiction necessarily implies: the attempt to enclose a God who is not of this world, an essentially eschatological divine act, within the history of a determined people in the world. And this is because "the only thing that can have prophetical value for man is the failure of his own ways and his recognition that it is impossible for him in his intra-mundane history to enter into direct possession of God and to identify his intra-mundane history with the act of God."

The Old Testament becomes revelation or the Word of God for the Christian who finds in it the tragic disavowal of the human project to appropriate God.[29]

But it is quite clear that the Old Testament is never in itself all this. It is, only "in a mediate way" [30] with faith in Christ as its basis and point of departure, a faith which subsists independently of it. And this is why the Old Testament is not rigorously indispensable for Christians. Reading the Old Testament brings nothing to the believer's faith which it does not already substanially possess.[31] And the various New Testament writings do not all refer to it to the same degree. There are even some that do not refer to it at all, and others that do not recall it in any way.[32] This merely confirms *de facto* what a simple reflection on the nature of true eschatological faith can alone enable us to establish.

It is not only the results of criticism and the seriousness of science which forbid us to see in the Old Testament a marvelous book of extraordinary oracles in which we can recognize—either immediately, or by means of the artifices of allegorical exegesis—the very finger of God. It is also fundamentally faith itself that prevents us from considering it in this way. This is because to do so would be to try to find a support external to this faith thus betraying the very nature of faith itself. Far from preparing or introducing faith, all the artificial procedures of exegesis that try to solicit or found it by means of the marvels they invoke can, in

29 Cf. *G.V.* II, pp. 183-86; I, pp. 335-36.
30 *G.V.* I, p. 335.
31 Cf. *ibid.*, p. 334.
32 Cf. *ibid.*, p. 336.

reality, only obscure and obliterate it.[33] Once faith has entered into the heart of man, it can appropriate the Old Testament like any other reality. But, as much for deciding itself as for confirming itself, it doesn't need the Old Testament any more than it needs any other reality in the world.

Critical Reflections

Some critics have felt that they have discovered a certain Marcionism in Bultmann's thought.[34] What we described above at least indicates that this judgment should be understood with certain nuances. His theology certainly has a very marked tendency to depreciate the Old Testament.

Bultmann himself has underlined the importance of the fact that the primitive Christian community kept the Old Testament as a holy book. Bultmann remarks that if it is true that the Judaeo-Christian communities were tempted to consider themselves merely as a new sect with Judaism, the temptation that plagued the Hellenistic communities was quite the opposite: they tended to consider themselves a "new religion" existing alongside of both Paganism and Judaism and distinguished from both of them by an essential progress in the order of knowledge of God and of the moral ends they pursued. The possession of the Old Testament was to be the most precious counterweight to this too natural tendency. "According to the Old Testament, in fact, God is not the law of the world that reveals itself to thought and to research, but the God who reveals himself in history." The Old Testament constituted the best resistance against any project to elaborate a "natural theology," and such projects rapidly appeared. "Thanks to the Old Testament, the idea that God reveals himself in what he *does* was conserved, and it is only from this point of departure that the person of Jesus and his cross can be understood. It is from this that we can and should understand what is an eschatological event, if it is true that it should not be characterized as a mythological

---

[33] Cf. *G.V.* I, p. 335; II, pp. 167-68; *Th.N.T.*, p. 116.
[34] One of these authors is J. B. Soucek, in *K.M.* IV, p. 26.

event." The Old Testament also furnished a reply to any elaboration of a "natural morality" centered on an idea of personal virtue and perfection. It defined, rather, the meaning of a truly religious ethic in which the Good is nothing other than the expression of the concrete exigencies of God's will.[35]

But can't we ask once more [36] whether Bultmann has underestimated the dangers to a Christianity which has no more than a fragile and purely occasional link with history? And doesn't his attitude toward the Old Testament bear many consequences in this regard?

There is no doubt that the Old Testament always has been and should be distinguished from the New. But our faith sees it as more than a human treasure, precious but unessential. The reason is, first of all, that it is more than a particularly striking illustration of the antithesis that the Law represents to the Gospel. It furnishes, as we said, the "material" from which the Gospel itself is "woven." [37] It is true that it is only beginning with the New Testament that we can discover all the meaning and the full scope of what the Old Testament announced and prefigured. As for the New Testament, it never reveals itself but as the accomplishment and transfiguration of the Old Testament. Bultmann recognized that the passage from one Testament to the other somehow expresses the very movement of our faith. But we do not think that this faith does anything else but appropriate to itself the objective act by which the Lord of the world and of history revealed all of his faithfulness and accomplished all of his promises. The reason is that before these promises are realized on the level of my act of faith, they were realized once for all and in fullness in the mystery of the life, death and resurrection of Jesus. If, as Bultmann concedes, we can reread the Old Testament and hear it speaking about Jesus,[38] it is not only because any reality, after a while, can tend to express a faith that is already believed; it is first

---

[35] *Th.N.T.*, pp. 116-18. Cf. *New Testament Studies* (1954), I, p. 10.
[36] Cf. *supra*, p. 73.
[37] H. de Lubac, *Histoire et Esprit* (Paris, 1950), p. 381; cf. *ibid.*, p. 383. In the same direction, cf. J. Levie, "Les limites de la preuve d'Ecriture sainte" in *Nouvelle Revue Théologique* (1949), pp. 1012-14.
[38] Cf. *G.V.* I, p. 336.

and essentially because Jesus assumed it after having made it so, so to speak, by his own body, and because he revealed all of its mysterious meaning when he delivered his body to the cross and diffused his Spirit on our world. It seems to us that Bultmann's theology has once again emptied the cross of Jesus, this Easter and this Pentecost, of part of its content. It is impossible to respect the totality of the mystery of our salvation without retaining, along with the divine wonders to which it introduces us (Bultmann's "eschatological" realities), the human and historical realities in which it revealed itself and which it transfigures, but without purely and simply reabsorbing them.[39]

In this way, the Old Testament authors could announce positively—though in a manner veiled to their contemporaries and even to themselves—the coming and the destiny of Jesus. It is true that Jesus puts an "end" to this history of salvation which was confused with the history of a carnal people and to the "pedagogy" by which God had prepared Israel progressively to recognize the gift of himself in the person of his Son which he would make to it. But is this opposed to the expected and promised Messiah represented as the "end" of a long historical process, since he is considered as much in the eyes of faith as in a general reflection on history? Wasn't it as the authentic offspring of the chosen people that he was truly to become Savior? We certainly must not confuse the believer's point of view with that of the philosopher or the man who is simply historian. We cannot establish the reality of Jesus' messianic character or of his fulfillment of the prophecies as we can establish a truth of pure science. But can't a simple objective study of Scripture prepare the decision of faith and, after a while, give it a very reasonable justification? The traditional "argument from the prophecies," whatever the variety of forms it takes, does retain its apologetical and theological value.

It is the mysterious accomplishment of the whole of the Old Testament, effectively accomplished in Jesus Christ, which gives a

[39] According to Bultmann, at the point where the New Testament message is expressed in all its purity, history is completely swallowed up into eschatology. Cf. *New Testament Studies* (1954), I, p. 11.

truly historical foundation to "allegorical" exegesis. And Bultmann undoubtedly misunderstands its most authentic realizations.[40] It is true that it has been abused, and that the literal sense from which we should never detach ourselves has often been too easily set aside. But once we have made the minimum of effort necessary to suppress the obstacles that inhere in undeniable cultural differences, can we quite seriously relegate the exegeses of an Origin, a Gregory of Nyssa, or an Augustine, to the rank of childishness and untenable fantasies? Wouldn't we also have to eliminate or completely depreciate the innumerable examples of "allegorical" exegesis with which the New Testament furnishes us and in line with which—with a striking sense of Scripture, despite the interpretations of details that do not satisfy us—the Fathers' exegesis faithfully situates itself? (Bultmann does not hesitate to make arbitrary choices in his exegesis.[41]

We realize, however, that it is not only for reasons of criticism or science that Bultmann rejects everything that could lead us to give meaning or too great a value to the Old Testament. He does it entirely in the name of that purely "eschatological" faith which he thinks defines the Gospel's own proper contribution. It is because he wants to affirm the transcendence and absolute newness of the revelation accomplished in Jesus Christ that Bultmann feels it is necessary to emphasize that the Old Testament is definitively ended and that any meaning it still has in the order of faith can only be "mediate" and negative. However, by a circle of events, it is this very transcendence and newness which are, in turn, endangered. According to Bultmann, the newness of the New Testament has nothing to do with a development of religious consciousness. At least, for him, such a consideration has nothing to do with faith, and it has no real theological meaning. The clearest and most open minds of the Old Testament could, in fact, have *hoped* for a future containing everything which we now *believe* has been

---

[40] Regarding the different formulas which can serve to designate this "allegorical" exegesis, and regarding the different meanings which can be attributed to the word "allegory," cf. H. de Lubac, *Histoire et Esprit,* pp. 384ff.

[41] Cf. *infra,* p. 103.

realized with the coming of Jesus.[42] The transcendence and newness of Christian faith consist solely in the recognition of this *now*.[43]
They imply no new knowledge of God. But can we say, therefore, that our situation has really changed in comparison with that
of the Jews? Perhaps salvation is *signified* to us in a different way
than it was to them: it comes to us through the scandal of the
cross of Jesus, instead of through the failures and contradictions in
an impossible history. The relation with God instituted by Christian faith is as much beyond all the realities that express our
existence, as it was for the Jews. The reality of salvation is yet to
come.

Is it true that the entire content of the New Testament can be
reduced to the fact that it notifies us of this eschatological *now*
linked with the appearance of Jesus? At the same time as it is an
actual message of salvation, isn't the New Testament the living
manifestation of a person? And when Jesus accomplished the messianic hope of Israel, wasn't he, in a sense, revealing it to itself? [44]
He brought an entirely new light to bear on his mission, and this
light found its source in the intimacy of his messianic consciousness (the existence of which Bultmann denies [45]). And this is
precisely what the New Testament authors were trying to communicate to us all through their work. It is this light which already
was troubling to Jesus' contemporaries and caused them to marvel
or to lose themselves in darkness. And it is this light which continues to make men responsible for their option in face of the
Gospel. And doesn't this light enable us to penetrate further than
was ever possible to any just man in the Old Testament: to pene-

---

[42] "To the degree that the idea of God was thought in a radical way in
Israel because the idea of sin and of grace was grasped in a radical way, the
Old Testament faith is hope, and in face of it, the New Testament faith
appears as faith which contains the accomplishment" (*G.V.* I, p. 331).

[43] Cf. *G.V.* I, pp. 204, 265, etc.

[44] "Before the time when we could actually know who Christ is, it was
impossible to obtain an adequate idea of what he was to be . . . The light
which Christ brought with him by his very presence not only clarified his
identity but also, so to speak, his essence" (H. de Lubac, *op cit.*, pp.
441-42).

[45] Cf. *Th.N.T.*, pp. 26-33. Cf. *supra*, p. 73.

trate not only into the mystery of the Messiah, but also into the mystery of a love which is God himself? [46]

In fact, the mystery of Jesus does not only announce to us the act of a forgiveness which calls us from all our sinful existence. This act is already really accomplished in him, because he lived it effectively in his body of flesh. The real principle of the new world is not only Christ's message or Word; it is also his body. There is no denying that this passage from a merely signified revelation to an effectively realized incarnation, and an already consummated Easter, is repugnant to Bultmann. The sacrament of this gift which God really gave us of himself and of this Easter, in which he invites us to participate from now on, is the body of Jesus Christ delivered up to the cross. Our faith is nourished on his body but, at the same time, also on *all* of Scripture which can reveal to us its boundless treasures.

[46] After he has described the direction of Luther's Christology, which was less concerned with knowing the internal mystery of Christ than with hearing his promises and the sovereign call of his voice, Y. Congar underlines the "Semitic, prophetical, biblical" character of this viewpoint. But he adds that it is, therefore, necessary to think about the Old Testament because "it is evident that the internal mystery of God, which up to that time had hardly been glimpsed at, was revealed with Jesus Christ, and that faith, from that time on, attained a new dimension of knowledge" ("La Christologie de Luther" in *Das Konzil von Chalkedon* III [Würzburg, 1954], p. 483).

CHAPTER FIVE

The New Testament Church*

According to Bultmann, the New Testament begins, strictly speaking, not with the manifestation and preaching of Jesus, but with the paschal event, understood especially as the beginning of apostolic kerygma. He underlines in his *Theology of the New Testament* that Jesus' preaching—and what interests Bultmann in Jesus is essentially his Word—depends on the "presuppositions" of a New Testament theology, which is not properly part of it.[1] This preaching, as a development of the act of Christian faith, could not become a reality until the moment when he who had been the "bearer of the message" became its "essential content." [2]

In this way, Bultmann deliberately places the New Testament in the environment where it was lived, preached, believed in, understood and formulated: in the midst of the primitive community. He had already done this once before according to the procedures of Form-Criticism in his *History of the Synoptic Tradition*. But he does it more completely and more synthetically in the

* This chapter appeared in "Aux origines de l'Eglise," *Recherches bibliques* VII (Desclée de Brouwer, 1965).
[1] *Op. cit.*, p. 1.
[2] *Ibid.*, p. 34.

Theology of the New Testament, which is undoubtedly the most remarkable of his works.

In this latter work, he brings together all of his research and intuitions to form one complete whole over which he never loses control. And in this work, he presents us with the history of the primitive community. He gives us not only the history of its formulas and representations but also, through them, the history of the understanding, which it had or took from itself, of its faith, of the message which it knew how to live, and of the mission which it had to fulfill. It is a history of the variations that the different places and times had of the Christian reality that is deposited in the New Testament.

The Primitive Community

According to Bultmann, the very first community, in the days that followed the paschal event, continued at first to live and think to a considerable degree within the framework of Jewish apocalyptic thought. Extending Jesus' preaching, it announced, not his return, but his coming as Messiah, the Son of Man. However, it already understood and proclaimed the resurrection of Jesus as the proof that he who had been crucified was elevated to the messianic role of the Son of Man. Quickly and ever increasingly, this event of the resurrection came to be considered the decisive event. And the primitive community itself became ever more conscious that it was the eschatological community—though this consciousness was more one of practice than of reflection. It felt that as such it was animated by the Spirit and already living under the radiance of him whom God had glorified, and it did not take long to see in him the "Messiah," the "Son of David," the "Son" or "Servant of God." Its congregating at Jerusalem, the practice of baptism, the eucharistic meal, etc., give very certain witness to this consciousness which the first community had that it was the "eschatological" community.

The spreading of the faith and kerygma to Hellentistic circles was a very important moment in the history of the primitive community. This propagation occurred very early, since it was the point from which Paul developed his own kerygma and theology. The preaching of Hellenistic Judaism had opened the way to the pagan world for the Christian missionaries, and it had already borrowed certain things from the thought patterns of the world into which it penetrated. The newly constituted communities were faced not only with the old problem of their relation to the pagan world, but they had the new problem regarding what attitude to take and what judgment to make in face of the strong Judaizing tendencies in the older Palestinian community. It fell to Paul to solve these problems in all their depth, and, in doing so, he brought to light what the new faith was in reality and what the community was as defined by it.

However, the Hellenistic communities, without waiting any longer, began to state their faith in terms of the surrounding cultural world, and this left its mark, in particular, on the way in which the person and work of Jesus is presented. He became the *Kyrios,* the object of cult. His title, "Son of God," became understood as characterizing his nature. The sacraments of baptism and the eucharist were interpreted by analogy with mysticism and the cult of the mystery religions. Finally, on a more speculative plane, when they were faced by such an important movement as Gnosticism, the young Christian communities tried to show the radical originality of their message, and they could not help but make large borrowings from Gnosticism on the level of expression.

According to Bultmann, Paul furnished a brilliant expression for the kerygma which elaborated itself little by little in the heart of the Hellenistic communities. John later furnished a brilliant expression for the kerygma elaborated—and he himself contributed greatly to its formulation—in the Christian communities of the East.

Bultmann feels that if we are to interpret these two great theologies correctly, we must distinguish between "what is said" and "what is meant." He sees in these two theologies a remarkably developed expression of the true eschatological faith that corresponds to the New Testament accomplishment of the Word of grace and salvation. We come across these theologies again, a little later on, when we are looking to discover what our author considers to be the authentic New Testament ecclesiology. But, beforehand, we must indicate a final stage in this evolution that we have undertaken to describe.

This faith, which, according to Bultmann, took a certain amount of time to disengage itself in all its purity and all its force and newness, and whose formulation culminated in the Pauline and Johannine theologies, did not take long to degrade itself in a fatal way by falling back more or less to the carnal level of Judaism and the pagan religions. Bultmann is not afraid to read in the New Testament itself the witness to this return to the world. More than one New Testament book manifests the progressive corruption of the eschatological perspectives to which the Pauline and Johannine theologies had born testimony. And Bultmann calls this corruptive movement the "evolution toward the ancient Church," and it furnishes the object for the third part of his *Theology of the New Testament.*

Bultmann says it is quite evident that during its development, the Church was brought to define more precisely a certain juridical order to rule its phenomenal existence. The most urgent question posing itself regarded the very meaning of this order. Was it to have a merely "regulatory" character? Was it to result solely from the power of faith or from the "Spirit" that animated the community? Or should there be conferred upon it a "constitutive" character, that would consider the Church the organism through which grace is communicated and thus become the "institution of salvation?" Without doubt, the question was never posed so neatly. And in reality, in all the practical answers which we find even in the New Testament, we can discover all possible nuances, and we can note all the changes of emphasis and all the undeniable contradictions.

Bultmann entertains no doubts regarding the direction of the evolution as a whole. The charism is more and more connected with the function, and they come to think that it can be transmitted by a rite. The title, *Apostolos,* which had first designated all the missionaries of the Gospel (and still does in Paul's writings), soon came to be reserved to the Twelve who were considered to be the guarantees of tradition and the leaders of the Church. It no longer seemed sufficient that the power of the Spirit assures the continuity of this tradition or the unity of the Church. Rather, they were made to depend on an institutionally regulated succession. Simultaneously, sacraments and ecclesiastical ordinances were more and more looked upon as the organs or means by which the goods and truths of salvation are transmitted. The last stage of this evolution, which manifests its direction admirably, was the institution of the penitential discipline. This was conceived to be a kind of repetition of baptism, and it was given sacramental value, in the fact that it expressed the exercise of the Church's jurisdiction.

To all of these transformations in the Church there naturally corresponded a new understanding of its own reality. The "eschatological" character of the Church was no longer understood to be the ever renewed relation with God constituted by the wonderful work of the Word of reconciliation; rather, it came to be understood as the present "possession" of institutions which can themselves communicate the goods of the beyond. The *tension* that was characteristic of primitive eschatology became more and more reduced, and the end of times withdrew into the indeterminate future: they were naturally brought to arrange themselves with the world. Already in more than one way, faith began to transform itself into "bourgeois Christian piety." Christianity was considered to be a new religion, following upon or alongside of Judaism and the various paganisms. The history of salvation continues and becomes identified with that of the Church. Luke already bears witness to this new way of seeing things. However, in order to illustrate this point, besides the New Testament authors, Bultmann also calls upon the early Christian authors (Ignatius of Antioch, Clement of Rome, *Didache,* etc.).

But what does Bultmann understand to be this Church to which he continually refers? How does he understand it in terms of the New Testament? The New Testament presents us with quite diverse conceptions of what the Church is, and we can certainly discern lines of evolution. At its heart, however, or at its summit, at the limit of its pure message, Bultmann thinks that it witnesses to a well-determined understanding of the Church. And it is this understanding that we will now consider.

The Church in the New Testament

The idea which best enables us to summarize everything that Bultmann considers to be the true Church of the New Testament is that of "eschatological" community. And to affirm that the Church is the eschatological community is to affirm that it has its reality at the limit, at the "end," of the world. As such, the Church is in no way the work of men. It can never enter into their possession. They can never in any way arrange or regulate it. The Church always comes to be, by the grace of God, where "the Word of reconciliation" is announced.

This is why it is constituted above all as the "community of cult." It is in cult that the Lord is present. And this presence becomes effective, in the power of the Spirit, by the proclamation of the Word that simultaneously carries the Church forth and proceeds from it. Even if the Christian community can be called the Church outside of its cultual gatherings, it is the cultual assembly that manifests its true essence, and the community's whole life is dominated by it.

Always gathered together by the Word of its Lord which is proclaimed and heard in faith during the assembly's practice of cult, the Church can equally be understood as "the community of the elect," and this is its third fundamental characteristic. It is not a society of persons who possess the truths or means of salvation; rather, it is the community of those whom the Word of grace has overtaken and whom it ever continues to overtake.[3]

Therefore, according to Bultmann, is the true Church of the New Testament a purely invisible Church? It is, rather, both visible and invisible. This Church which proceeds completely from the Word of God and his grace is realized effectively in our world and in our history. The Lord whom it venerates in its cult is not only "he who is to come" but also, identically, he who has already come and who has called into existence this community that has assembled in his name. But this historical realization should never be isolated from the transcendent, "eschatological" act which it expresses and which cannot subsist naturally in the world. The invisible character of the Church in its reality is not that of an "idea,"

[3] Cf. *G.V.* I, pp. 164ff.

but "that of an eschatological event, intelligible only to faith, which occurs ever anew within history." [4] Bultmann further explains that, like the cross of Christ upon which it is founded, the Church is an "ambiguous phenomenon": "visible like a fact of the world, invisible—though at the same time visible to the eyes of faith—as a reality of the world to come." [5]

What Bultmann is trying to bring into relief is that the Church, according to the most authentic New Testament message, is always essentially constituted from above by a continual, or rather, ever renewed, intervention of God, which is neither perceived nor received except in faith. This transcendence—which Bultmann calls the "eschatological" character or the relation to the future—is retained only to the measure that the Church understands itself as the Church of the Word, the bearer of the Word, because the Church is constituted by the Word.

We have already emphasized that Bultmann is far from opposing Scripture to the Church. Still less does he oppose the Church to the Word (which he does not fail to distinguish from Scripture). Not only does he not oppose them, but he feels that we are never considering them in their truth when we consider them independently of each other. The Church is constituted by the Word because it is by the Word that salvation is continually made present and the true community of faith, the new Israel, is built. But inversely, and just as really, the Word doesn't exist except by the Church. It is the Word that, "not by its non-temporal signifying content, but as an authorized preaching, is transmitted by a tradition." [6] The preacher is as much "servant" of the Word as he is "servant" of the Church.[7] Both the Church and the Word express the same "eschatological" intervention of God.

If there is an opposition that dominates Bultmann's thought, it is not one between the Word and the Church; rather, it is an opposition between a Church of the Word and a Church of the Sacrament. This does not mean that he ignores the place which the sacraments occupied in the life of the New Testament communi-

---

[4] *Ev. Joh.*, p. 394.
[5] *Th.N.T.*, p. 304.
[6] *G.V.* I, p. 181.
[7] *Ibid.*, pp. 180-81.

ties, but he does tend to minimize their importance, particularly in his interpretation of John's gospel. He feels that in those parts of the New Testament where they are looked upon in their true meaning, the sacraments are nothing more than a *verbum visibile* in the strict sense of the word: "They do no more than the Word does. Like the Word, they actualize the act of salvation . . . This is why Paul could designate the Lord's Supper as a preaching" (1 Cor. 11, 26).[8] What Bultmann dreads, and what he already sees outlined in the New Testament itself, is, as we have mentioned, the idea of a Church that is an "institution of salvation" in which the sacraments are taken to be organs or administrative means, sources of grace which the Church itself can manage.

Bultmann feels that there is serious danger in Paul's description of the Church as the "body of Christ"; Paul tried to use this in his attempt to express the transcendence of the Church. Without doubt, the doctrine can be correctly interpreted, if we read in it the conviction that the Church is always constituted by its Lord who precedes every assembly of those who are "in him," like the great Church always precedes the particular Churches in which it manifests itself and finds its realization. The danger is that this Church might not identify itself purely and simply with Christ and might consider itself as possessing the goods of salvation which, in reality, can only come ever anew by the Word and the grace of God. For Bultmann, a Church of the Sacrament is a Church that has lost its understanding of the "eschatological" character of salvation. It is a Church that no longer allows itself to be lifted up by God who comes and reserves to himself the calling of the elect. It is a Church that thinks it has the right to administer his Spirit and his gifts. By the very fact, such a Church becomes—or remains— simply a manifestation of the sinful world.

Critical Reflections

Here as elsewhere, Bultmann is to be criticized more for what he excludes than for what he values. We do not want to reject this eschatological dimension of the New Testament Church upon

[8] *Ibid.,* p. 181.

which he insists so much and which the Catholic Church has perhaps too often lost sight of. The Church is not only "Jesus Christ continued"; it is not simply "in possession of" the Holy Spirit; it is not simply built on the rock once for all and equipped, so to speak, with everything necessary to bring men to salvation. In a sense, it does remain "at the mercy" of God, without, however, doubting his fidelity to accomplish in it what he promised. The Church never ceases to receive from him who remains its Head and Savior. Neither can it ever separate itself from the Word, because it is the Word that recalls to the Church its origin and founds it in its faith. And all these aspects of the mystery of the Church are affirmed in the New Testament.

We must recognize a number of differences in emphasis in the ecclesiology of the various New Testament books and authors, and we can see lines of evolution. For example, P. Benoit has demonstrated the existence of such an evolution, or rather of such a development, within the Pauline doctrine of the Church as the body of Christ.[9] In the same way, in his excellent work of biblical theology, *Règne et Royaume de Dieu*,[10] R. Schnackenburg has analyzed the undeniable evolution of New Testament eschatology, in its relation to the idea of royalty, of reign, or of the kingdom of God. So, Bultmann can encourage us ever increasingly to nuance our presentation of New Testament ecclesiology.

But what we refuse to give Bultmann is the right to set up certain aspects of this ecclesiology as the absolute norm and to represent as illegitimate everything else which, in reality, deepens or complements these aspects. Why should the concrete and very complex mystery of the Church have been revealed and constituted all at once and have been adequately expressed only by means of certain Pauline perspectives? Bultmann considers the sayings about the Church which the gospels attribute to Jesus to be purely redactions. Even without referring to Jesus' prophetic consciousness, what we know about the religious world of the time, particularly since the Qumran discoveries, suffices to convince us that there is nothing impossible or aberrating in these declarations. And

[9] Cf. "Corps, tête et plérôme dans les Epîtres de la captivité" in *R.B.* (1956), pp. 5-44.
[10] Paris, 1965.

why shouldn't the Church, far from degenerating, have solidified and extended and even enriched its understanding of itself, so that the concepts in the pastoral epistles and in the Book of Revelation necessarily must be integrated in a total presentation of New Testament ecclesiology? They must be integrated, not merely juxtaposed. They must be grasped in a view which "comprehends" the different "datums" sufficiently for it to be evident that it is always the same mystery which is delivered to us under different aspects or in different "moments" of its manifestation. Such a work—perhaps never to be accomplished—is certainly more difficult than building a system around one aspect. But this work imposes itself on anyone who wants to remain faithful to the New Testament.

The direction of Bultmann's systematization can be explained in part by the anthropology or philosophical views inherent in it. He certainly proceeds from a too individualistic conception of man and of history to account for the mystery of the Church in a satisfying way. Nevertheless, he knows that even Paul to whom he is continually referring—like Jesus before him, in his preaching—"never sees man as an isolated individual . . . For Paul, man finds himself, in the beginning and always, in a historical context. . . ." [11] This is why Bultmann does not want to consider the Word of God and the work of grace independently of the Church and a certain tradition. However, he always tends to look upon this reality as a simple "matter" to which the individual alone can give meaning.

Bultmann's theology of the Church is dominated above all by a certain idea of the manner of God's presence and action in his revelation and grace. And we can once again refer to this manner as exclusively prophetical. We have already described how strongly Bultmann defends a Church of the Word against a Church of the Sacrament. It is not as if this repugnance were spontaneous and relatively superficial as that of a Protestant theologian toward the hierarchical and sacerdotal institution in which the Roman Church is too easily assimilated. Bultmann's ecclesiology is predetermined by his Christology. And in his Christology, from the viewpoint of the history of salvation, Jesus is identified with his Word; Jesus is nothing else than the "eschatological Word of reconcil-

[11] *G.V.* I, p. 168.

iation.[12] From this, his body of flesh born of a woman, and all the extent of time during which he performed his mission, lose most of their profound meaning. And so do his *acta et passa in carne* on which the sacramental system and the apostolic ministry are constructed. This is because the apostolic ministry is not only the preaching of the paschal kerygma; it is the ministry of men whom Jesus himself chose and *established,* after having made himself known to them by a long familiarity, so that they might remain witnesses and faithful guardians to his memory and his work. And he did not begin this work only on the day of Easter; he placed its foundations during his mortal life before confirming it on the cross.

Proceeding from a contracted idea of Jesus' person and work, Bultmann can only give an equally narrow and partial presentation of the New Testament Church. There are many images through which the mystery of the Church is revealed to us in Scripture: the temple of God, the body of Christ, the spouse, etc. And this multiplicity indicates the inexhaustibility of this mystery.[13] We have noticed the reserve with which Bultmann receives the fundamental doctrine that the Church is the body of Christ. This reserve is certainly significant. No less serious in meaning and consequence is his neglect of the doctrine of the Church as spouse of Christ, as it is formulated in the fifth chapter of the Epistle to the Ephesians or in Rev. 21, 2. 9. Bultmann is satisfied to mention Eph. 5, 25 in the midst of a list of "Gnostic themes." [14] But this doctrine involves a concept of the relation between God and his work of salvation which is anything but a pure event. For this reason, it could be embarrassing to Bultmann. The image of the Church as the spouse of Christ expresses God's absolute sovereignty over his work, but it also expresses that God is *well pleased* with it. In opposition to the transcendentalism of Bultmann's ecclesiology which, in reality, limits the power of divine love, this image manifests what we might call the dialogical structure of revelation and the redemption. In no other way can we understand the whole meaning of the mystery of the Church.

[12] Cf. *supra,* pp. 59-61.
[13] Cf. especially the conciliar *Constitution on the Church,* n. 6.
[14] Cf. *Th.N.T.,* p. 178.

Epilogue

In response to numerous criticisms coming from his fellow Protestants with regard to his project of demythologizing (in which he had summarized all his work), Bultmann retorted that "radical demythologizing is parallel to the Pauline and Lutheran doctrine of justification by faith alone without the works of the Law." Or rather, he went on, "it is the realization which is its consequence in the domain of consciousness. Like the doctrine of justification, it destroys every false assurance and every false desire for assurance which man can have, whether this assurance is based upon his good works or whether it is based upon a solid understanding of his ascertainments. A man who wants to believe in God as his God should know that he holds nothing in his hands on which he can support his faith, and that he must remain suspended in air and can claim no justification for the Word that is addressed to him." [1]

On the other hand, Karl Barth feels that in order to understand Bultmann, it is good to recall that he is Lutheran and that the question of *applicatio salutis* is of primary importance in Lutheranism. And from it is derived the question regarding the believing subject.[2]

Therefore, a Catholic might be tempted to attribute purely and simply to the Christianity descended from the Reformation all of

[1] Cf. *K.M.* II, p. 207.
[2] Cf. Karl Barth, "Rudolf Bultmann" in *Versuch, ihn zu verstehen* (Zürich, 1953), pp. 46-48.

105

the gaps and ineptitudes which he can find in the theology of the Marburg exegete.

It is true that in more than one way, Bultmann is in the "logic" of Protestantism when he detaches faith from the historical or psychological elements in which it is rooted and transmitted or, in other words, when he gives in to the idealist temptation or, at least, when he is unable to fully accept an incarnate revelation along with a prophetical one. But we know, too, how the unilateral development of a certain Catholic "logic," distinguished especially by an anti-Protestantism, can engender deficient and disputable positions. The faith of the Churches cannot be reduced to these "logics."

Neither can we content ourselves with seeing in Bultmann a peril that must be exorcised from the Christian world. This dauntless theologian has alerted us to the urgency of problems we cannot avoid. By the radical character of the solutions which he proposes (with the merit that they are well thought out), he provokes every confession to enter into renewed contact with the very foundations of the faith it claims. This is why we think that the "crisis" in Christian consciousness to whose formulation Bultmann greatly contributed, and that he even precipitated, should not be simply deplored in a sterile manner. Rather, it should convince all the Churches of the renewed urgency of the theological task.